DARWIN'S ANGEL

A Seraphic Response to *The God Delusion*

JOHN CORNWELL

PROFILE BOOKS

This paperback edition published in 2008

First published in Great Britain in 2007 by
Profile Books Ltd
3A Exmouth House
Pine Street
Exmouth Market
London EC1R 0JH
www.profilebooks.com

1 3 5 7 9 10 8 6 4 2

Designed and typeset in Venetian 301 by MacGuru Ltd
info@macguru.org.uk

Printed in the UK by CPI Bookmarque, Croydon, CR0 4TD

A CIP catalogue record for this book is available from the British Library.

ISBN 978 1 84668 065 6

Mixed Sources
Product group from well-managed
forests and other controlled sources
www.fsc.org Cert no. TT-COC-002227
© 1996 Forest Stewardship Council
FSC

"Monkeys make men. Men make angels."
Charles Darwin (Notebook B)

"… we are not angels, who view the universe from the outside. Instead, we and our models are both part of the universe we are describing."
Stephen Hawking ("Gödel and the End of Physics", Paper available on the Web)

Contents

	Preface	9
1.	A Summary of Your Argument	21
2.	Your Sources	29
3.	Imagination	33
4.	Beauty	37
5.	What is Religion?	43
6.	Is God Supernatural?	47
7.	Celestial Teapots	53
8.	God's Simplicity	59
9.	Theories of Everything	63
10.	Dawkins versus Dostoyevsky	69

11. Jesus, the Jews, and the "Pigs"   77

12. Dawkins's Utopia   85

13. Fundamentalism   93

14. Is Religious Education Child Abuse?   99

15. Life after Death   111

16. Religious People Less Clever than Atheists?   117

17. Does Our Moral Sense Have a Darwinian Origin?   125

18. The Darwinian Imperative   129

19. Religion as a Bacillus   137

20. Does God Exist?   147

21. Being Religious   157

    Acknowledgments   167

Preface

One of the most beautiful conceits of mortal wit is the idea of the angel; for angels exemplify, symbolise, and render intelligible the dynamic mental capacity known as imagination. "Angels," according to Thomas Aquinas, the medieval theologian and philosopher, "exist anywhere their powers are applied … The angel is now here, now there, with no time-interval between." And since angels are conceived as operating outside, as well as within, space and time, it is not surprising that the American poet Wallace Stevens should have characterised the creative imagination as "the necessary angel of earth" in whose sight one "sees the world again". And just as angels are free of the constraints of the physical universe, so the creative minds of gifted scientists are liberated from the laws of time, physics, and even logic, to make unifying connections between disparate elements of nature.

Conjure up suspension of disbelief, then, to imagine the presence of an angel special to natural historians and biologists. Consider, as if from the point of view of a guardian angel, the imagination of Charles Darwin on his famous voyage to the Galapagos, and his "discovery of the singular relations of the animals and plants inhabiting the several islands". Imagine, too, if you will, a guardian angel making connections between the minds of natural historians and biologists – from Darwin's day to this.

In his notebook Darwin wrote:

What a magnificent view one can take of the world. Astronomical causes, modified by unknown ones, cause changes in geography & changes of climate superadded to change of climate from physical causes, – then superadded changes of form in the organic world, as adaptation, & these changing affect each other, & their bodies by certain laws of harmony keep perfect in these themselves. – instincts alter, reason is formed, & the world peopled with myriads of distinct forms from a period short of eternity to the present time, to the future.

Back in London he wrote in his *Metaphysical Notebook*:

> my pleasure in Kensington Gardens has often been greatly
> excited by looking at trees [as] great compound animals
> united by wonderful mysterious manner. There is much
> imagination in every view. If one were admiring one in
> India, [and] a tiger stalked across the plains, how ones feel-
> ings would be excited, how the scenery would rise.

Imagination in modern science is dynamic, free, and yet con-
strained by widely accepted disciplines of enquiry; even more
so, in their own ways, are art and religion – which itself employs
every form of artistic imagination in its meditations, scriptures,
and practices. For what is religion if not a product of the imagination straining to connect everyday life with the transcendent
incarnate, the mystical? Not surprisingly the scientific and the
religious imagination find themselves at odds, in competition
even, especially in the realms of explanation, where both at times
trespass on each other's territories. It was precisely in response to
the "scientific" inferences drawn by fundamentalist religionists
of his day that Darwin pronounced evolution to be "far grander
than idea from cramped imagination that God created (warring
against those very laws he established in all … organic nature) the
Rhinoceros of Java [and] Sumatra that since the time of the Silu-
rian he has made a long succession of vile molluscous animals".

Darwin struggled, "with many fluctuations", between religious belief and doubt as he worked on his theory of evolution. Then he finally abandoned the Christian faith of his youth during the period between his return from the Galapagos and the publication of his great book, *On the Origin of Species*, adopting a belief in theism, a distant, unknown and unknowable, prime mover, in consequence of which "everything in nature is the result of fixed laws."

> Another source of conviction in the existence of God [he wrote in his *Autobiography*], connected with the reason and not with the feelings, impresses me as having much more weight. This follows from the extreme difficulty or rather impossibility of conceiving this immense and wonderful universe, including man with his capacity of looking far backwards and far into futurity, as the result of blind chance or necessity. When thus reflecting I feel compelled to look to a First Cause having an intelligent mind in some degree analogous to that of man; and I deserve to be called a Theist.

After the publication of the *Origin*, however, his theism surrendered to scepticism: "the mystery of the beginning of all things," he wrote, in his *Life and Letters*, "is insoluble by us; and I for one must be content to remain an Agnostic." It is significant that in this latter period Darwin found his sense of both the poetic and the scientific imagination also in decline. Echoing Coleridge's "Dejection: An Ode" ("I may not hope from outward forms to win / The passion and the life, whose fountains are within"), even the landscapes that once thrilled him now brought him no pleasure. The decline of his impression of the sublime appears to have been due to illness and depression. "My mind," he wrote in his *Autobiography*, "seems to have become a kind of machine for grinding general laws out of large collections of facts, but why this should have caused the atrophy of that part of the brain alone, on which the higher tastes depend, I cannot conceive." Yet for all his latter-day scepticism, at no time did Darwin suggest, in his private writings or in public, that religious belief was incompatible with the scientific imagination; nor did he judge religionists to be contemptible or dangerous.

Which brings me to one of Darwin's great contemporaries, a man in whom religion and science co-existed in tension, Father Gregor Mendel, who resided at the ancient Abbey at Brno, Moravia. Hence imagine me answering to the name Mendel's Angel, as to Darwin's, among other appellations, of which more below. In his cloister garden, employing different colours, shapes, and sizes of sweet pea, Father Mendel performed over many years those painstaking experiments that underpin theories to this day of genetic heredity. Since his death in obscurity more than a century ago, imagine me keeping an angelic eye on Father Mendel's garden while surveying the ever-turning wheel of science, and human history – with its triumphs and achievements, its conflicts and perils, its darkness and violence.

I kept watch in the cloisters at Brno during the momentous days of the Austro-Hungarian Empire, and its decline; then the years leading to Hitler's rise when the Gestapo oppressed Father Mendel's community. I was there, too, when on an inauspicious day the Abbey fell to the tyranny of the Soviets, who purged Father Mendel's work, imposing the pernicious science of Trofim Lysenko, who taught a version of Lamarckian inheritance of acquired characteristics. The monks were thrown in jail by their atheistic Communist oppressors, the sacred buildings rifled of their store of books and holy objects, the Abbey church commandeered as a storage site; Father Mendel's greenhouse, in use since his death, was smashed, the garden abandoned to weeds and brambles. Only after the fall of the Berlin Wall and the collapse of the Soviet Empire did the monks return, and the long-abandoned choir echoed once more to the sound of chanting.

⁓⸋⸘⸋⁓

Accompany me in your imagination, then, as I ring the earth in a trice, dropping in on laboratories, seminars, conferences, reading all those research papers and books. See me, today, in the first decade of the twenty-first century, proud to declare that I am now guardian of the brilliant popular expositor of zoology, Richard Dawkins, whom I strive to take as seriously as he takes himself. And his business is serious indeed, for he has called upon the faithless, the waverers, and even firm religious believers to follow him into radical atheism not merely as a private conviction but as a public profession. Religion, he insists, is the principal source of the world's evil.

In this he would seem to have a point. The Al Qaeda fanatics who perpetrated the 9/11 attacks were inspired by religious fundamentalism; so was the Zionist who massacred those worshippers in their West Bank mosque and the American Christian anti-abortionists who blew up clinics, slaughtering doctors and nurses. Fundamentalist religions of every kind are opposed in this century to democracy, religious freedom, pluralism, freedom of speech, a benign separation of state and religion. From stupid dogmas of creationism to ugly offences against the dignity of women, fundamentalism manifests itself through every world religion, including Islam, Christianity, Judaism, Hinduism, and Buddhism. Would not humankind be better off without religion, asks Professor Dawkins.

At the same time he seeks a more just world for atheists. They must "come out", he insists; profess courageously their convictions, or lack of them. Just as women, blacks, gays, and lesbians have demanded their human rights, he asks that atheists stand up and be counted. His slogan: "Atheist Pride!" He has yet to claim that there is a gene for atheism. To further his teachings he has established a charity, the Richard Dawkins Foundation for Reason and Science, a non-profit organisation for the mental and moral amelioration of the human race by means of the advancement of rationalism and humanism. He has established his own "Ten Commandments", and set up an "Official Richard Dawkins" website where his devotees can exchange views (www.RichardDawkins.net). And now he has sought to assign the status of religious non-affiliation even to the departed. He has un-faithed, or "outed" in eternity, such as Jefferson, Dostoyevsky, and Einstein; he has even "outed" my former protégé Father Mendel, who was so admirably a man of both science and religion.

Not so, Dawkins claims. "Mendel, of course ... was an Augustinian monk," he writes, " but that was in the nineteenth century, when becoming a monk was the easiest way for the young Mendel to pursue his science. For him, it was the equivalent of a research grant."

I must say that despite preternatural angelic intelligence I was unaware that men took the drastic step of entering monasteries in order to enjoy free scientific research funding. Not such a bad idea, though: one square meal a day (albeit frugal), a cell of your own, and endless leisure to pursue those long-term research programmes unencumbered by fleshly distractions. But what farsightedness! Father Mendel came to study plant biology late in his religious life, after seven years' philosophy and theology and a career as a teacher of general subjects. But I see the point the professor wants at all costs to make: that religious faith and science by definition cannot co-exist. We shall see.

By the same token Dawkins is reluctant to grant that religion can be in any circumstances a basis for human flourishing. There is no distinction, in his view, between tolerant religion and fundamentalism since all faith is against reason and therefore a source of ignorance, prejudice, and, ultimately, violence. And his campaign against faith comes at a time when religious observance in its many guises appears to be on the increase throughout the world, although not necessarily in terms of church attendance in Europe. This runs counter to those influential social thinkers of the nineteenth century who maintained that religion would retreat in the face of modern industrialised states. He reveals, by his vehemence, and impatience, that the process of predicted secularisation should be given a boost.

Understand that as Dawkins's guardian angel I am obliged to appreciate his point of view. Since he is utterly sincere in his beliefs, what possible moral harm can befall his immortal soul? Yet, one might object, there are religionists aplenty who feel threatened by his arguments. Well, the Almighty in his providence tests the faith of all, with every kind of trial. Humankind is meant to struggle for Heaven. In any case, why should Dawkins be not accorded the same respect for his convictions as any religionist? And having studied his book, and the reactions to it, I am convinced that his views may do more good than harm: what an explosion of reviews, viewpoints, newspaper columns, debates, lectures, and seminars he has prompted! What penetrating examination of convictions and confessions for both belief and atheism, with even the redoubtable, morally outraged Christopher Hitchens entering the fray with his *God is Not Great*! And it is not over yet. Hence in this journal-letter I intend not so much to pick a fight with the good professor as to offer a few "grace notes" and marginal glosses in the interests of sharper logic, closer insight, and factual accuracy, not so much to settle the debate as to stir it once more.

Dear Richard,

I

A Summary of Your Argument

After wrestling with religion and believers for years you've brought all your arguments for atheism to bear within the covers of one large volume, and copies of it have been swarming like so many flocks of little demons off the shelves of bookshops, supermarkets, and Amazon's depositories. Your characterisation of typical religious believers summons images of fanatical Muslims, Mid-Western evangelicals, Zionists, and Roman Catholic bigots. In your mind there is essentially no difference between an Al Qaeda terrorist and your North Oxford neighbour who goes to church twice a year. The mere fact of belief is the mechanism whereby religion morphs into murderous fanaticism.

The poet W. B. Yeats once wrote: "Hatred of God may bring the soul to God." For what many atheists loathe is not God but all those false representations, "the tinsel and trash" that obscure Him. The philosopher and novelist Iris Murdoch put the same point like this: "No existing thing could be what we have meant by God. Any existing God would be less than God. An existent God would be an idol or a demon." Hence what leads people to demolish false notions of God can bring them closer to God. As that other famous atheist Christian, the Anglican priest Don Cupitt, wrote: "The dissolution of God, and our attainment of perfect union with God, are one and the same thing." There is potential here for attainment to the highest levels of spirituality: the bracing mountain-top purity of a God beyond mortal description; purged of all human constructs. Such spiritual mountain-climbers are seldom popular. Think of the Great Jewish mystic Spinoza, or Islam's al-Hallaj, or the monk Meister Eckhart. All three were detested and persecuted by the defenders of organised religions: they found God by dismantling every last paltry doctrine of Him. Yet such dismantling of God, especially when it is attended by contempt of fellow human beings who continue to believe in Him according to their different fashions, can lead, as Iris Murdoch warned, to the substitution of a rival godhead. Idolatry. You intend, I know, substituting science for religion. But, as your guardian angel, I should hate to think that you are on the way to substituting *yourself* for God.

But allow me to begin by summarising *The God Delusion*. You insist that all claims for God's existence are "hypotheses about the universe", and therefore the exclusive province of science and reason – since our universe is all that is the case. So what of those purely rational, philosophical "proofs" for His existence that have been mulled over since the Middle Ages? What, in particular, of the argument for a Grand-Designer-God to solve the riddle of the order of the universe, and nature's exquisite, ordered complexities?

Following Charles Darwin's theory of evolution, you explain how the mystery of increasing complexity from the simplest life forms is sufficiently settled by the bottom-up, blind, non-purposive laws of evolution: natural selection. The key to evolution of species, as you explain, is replicators, or genes, which mutate by virtue of propensity to diversity or novelty. Those populations that find reproductive success or advantage within a given set of environments survive and thrive; but populations in environments unconducive to survival fail and decline. A similar circumstance obtains for human beings in the realm of culture, you claim. There are mental replicators you call memes, which spread like genes or viruses to the advantage or disadvantage of their host communities and societies. So, based remotely on Darwin's great idea, you have arrived at a theory for the growth of culture too, including, crucially, a theory about the development and spread of religions – which you consider a viral "infection". But you would go further. You would invoke Darwin, I see, for the origin of many universes, the so-called mother and daughter universes that reproduce on the same principle as natural selection. These many universes, according to a recent speculation, solve the problem of the "fine-tuned" universe that guaranteed the possibility of life on Earth. But I shall come back to that.

You then allow that anthropologists are competent to *describe* what religion is and what religionists do. But only Darwin's theory of evolution, you insist, can offer an *ultimate* explanation for the true *origins* of religion. So you proceed to relate what you believe to be a parallel in natural history.

A moth navigates by the light of the moon or the stars, but is sometimes attracted by the same conditioned reflexes into a candle-flame. These accidents of self-immolation, you tell your readers, are a "by-product" of a genetically determined behaviour that carries a survival advantage. Religion, you speculate, is a harmful by-product of the infant's disposition to believe parental myths. Believing in the big bad wolf in the woods may prevent a child straying. But accounts of those hell fires prepared for naughty children are received with the same credulity. Thus religious fictions that prompt fear, bigotry, hatred, and violence seize and imprison a child's psyche, and are passed on from generation to generation. And just as genes are biological replicators that drive the richness and diversity of nature, so too do the cultural replicators, the "memes" – habits of thought and behaviour, like beliefs, values, traditions, fashions, loyalties, and prejudices, that spread and form mental "populations". Memes of a religious nature, you contend, have consequences for all of us: beliefs in such doctrines as the afterlife, supernatural realities, heaven and hell, the immaterial soul, the superiority of one religion over another, and so forth lead inexorably to bigotry, divisions, hatred, and violence. For the good of humankind it is essential that people renounce the genetically established tendency to obey this dangerous by-product, religion, and all its beliefs, or "memes".

The tragedy for most believers, you contend, is their failure to understand that all are free to reject the religious indoctrination foisted upon them by their parents. You end with the heartening news that once God has been abandoned, "a proper understanding of the magnificence of the real world ... can fill the inspirational role that religion has historically – and inadequately – usurped."

Without commenting in depth on your main arguments at this point, it must be said at the outset, since Darwin's great idea is your central theme, that most sensible theologians have no problem with the theory of evolution. Being a religious believer is not synonymous with being a creationist – in other words, believing that the world and everything in it was literally created 5,000 years ago in six days by a patriarchal God in the sky. Most sensible modern religious believers accept, rather, that if God wanted to make the world in the way that Darwin proposes, why should he not? They are likely, however, to find problems with the way in which you apply Darwin's theory to social and cultural life: not least religion.

Then again, most human beings are capable of being moved both by nature and by the inward stirrings of the spirit without mutual exclusion. At times, in a great, mystical poet, such as William Wordsworth, an impulse to apprehend the sublime occurs both from outward nature and from the inner spirit, working in harmony. He characterised it as the "still, sad music of humanity".

> And I have felt
> A presence that disturbs me with the joy
> Of elevated thoughts; a sense sublime
> Of something far more deeply interfused,
> Whose dwelling is the light of setting suns,
> And the round ocean and the living air,
> And the blue sky, and in the mind of man;
> A motion and a spirit, that impels
> All thinking things, all objects of all thought,
> And rolls through all things …
>
> ('Lines composed a few miles above Tintern Abbey …)

But this is just an initial reaction. In such a large book with so many arguments and reflections we must take a little time to examine the leading points in greater depth.

2

Your Sources

Let me start by commenting briefly on the sources you have marshalled for a work that embraces science, philosophy, psychology, religion, spirituality, anthropology, sociology, history, and theology. Your book is as innocent of heavy scholarship as it is free of false modesty. I note that the author most often cited (both in the bibliography and in the text) is yourself – your own works, your own sayings, thought experiments, speculations, conversations with experts, and favourable opinions of your works by others. I was glad that you could quote the magnificent encomium of the late Douglas Adams (of *Hitchhiker's Guide to the Galaxy* fame) for your outspoken courage, which, you relate, you "never tire of sharing" with others. In the same way I loved your admission that Mrs Dawkins consented to read out loud to you *The God Delusion* in its 400-page entirety; not once but *twice*. How many professors could boast publicly of such uxorious devotion.

I should have liked some acknowledgment of the existence of William James, Max Weber, Emile Durkheim, Simone Weil, Martin Buber, and Karl Rahner. You might have discussed at least in brief your intellectual antecedents: Denis Diderot, Auguste Comte, Herbert Spencer, Karl Marx and Sigmund Freud. On Islam you rely heavily on, Ibn Warraq's *Why I am Not a Muslim* (an alternative, easier read might have been Salman Rushdie's *Satanic Verses*). Little or nothing on Judaism, Confucius, Buddhism, Hinduism, or Sufism. And in support of your many accessible excursions into anthropology you have read that fine old monument, Frazer's *Golden Bough*. On Christianity you mainly cite one philosopher of religion, Richard Swinburne.

What kind of book do you think you have written? Surely not a work of science. It has been noted by one reviewer (the scientist-theologian Dean of Jesus College, Cambridge) that the encomiums on the dust-jacket feature a line-up of writers in the realms of fantasy fiction (Philip Pullman), popular brain science (Steven Pinker), experimental pop music (Brian Eno), and conjuring tricks (Derren Brown). Does this help us locate you within a genre? The amalgam of styles is formidable:

preacher, teacher, consciousness-raiser, castigator, raconteur, propagandist, music, art, and literary critic, bar-room polemicist. It is essentially a dialogue with an invisible audience of fundamentalist religionist antagonists. But from time to time you become oracular, fielding answers to the kind of metaphysical "why?" questions irritatingly posed by five-year-olds. But I have no clear sense of you discriminating between history and theory, empirical evidence and intuition, statistical data and hunch. And I wonder, was it wise of you to claim that theology should not be regarded as an academic "subject" at all. Yet, in fairness, you do cite prominently a scientist who disagrees with you: the cosmologist Martin Rees. "The preeminent mystery," Rees has stated in *Our Cosmic Habitat*, "is why anything exists at all. What breathes life into the equations of physics, and actualized them in a real cosmos? Such questions lie beyond science, however: they are the province of philosophers and theologians." You dismiss this acknowledgment as folly. But we will return to that.

3

Imagination

You find theology, the study of God, meaningless, unworthy of a moment's serious study. In your view theologians are engaged in make-believe; the object of their investigations no more real than the Tooth Fairy. Compared with scientists, theologians in your view are mere fantasists. Yet while it is true that theology has its own special discourse, theologians draw on an impressive range of academic disciplines – including history, philosophy, anthropology, literary and scriptural criticism – and they bring together dynamic intellectual capacities – of the imagination. Some theologians, obviously, take a lead from "revelation", the possibility that God has spoken to human beings through His prophets and inspired writers of holy texts. Faith and revelation you dismiss out of hand, as you would, but you are also disturbed by the dimension of imagination, aren't you? It's so close to art, music, poetry — stuff that's made up rather than facts that can be reducible to physics, chemistry, and biology. You articulated your repudiation of imagination very plainly in an earlier work of yours, *Climbing Mount Improbable*.

In that book you describe how you attended a lecture about figs in poetry, religion, anthropology. "This kind of thing," you wrote, "is the stock-in-trade of a certain kind of literary mind, but it provokes me to literal mindedness." The "real poetry", the "real metaphor", lurking in the fig, you maintain, is its "Darwinian grammar and logic". Biology is true whereas the other stuff is just made up! It sounds as though you would substitute a set of case-notes on senile dementia for Shakespeare's *King Lear*; or a horticultural fact sheet for Wordsworth's "Daffodils". Elsewhere you permit a role for literature in a science-ruled utopia, provided that it is confined to anodyne tropes about "ineffable" sunsets and "sublime" landscapes. But your separation of fact and fiction, true and false, reality and imagination, science and everything else, could not be more plain. "The only difference between *The Da Vinci Code* and the gospels," you pronounce in your *God Delusion*, "is that the gospels are ancient fiction while *The Da Vinci Code* is modern fiction." That settles the hash of the four Evangelists, you maintain. *The Da Vinci Code*, which is not factual, is fiction; the Gospels are not factual (because they have all those factual inconsistencies, as you note), therefore the Gospels are fiction. So are you inviting your readers to infer that poets, dramatists, novelists are not concerned with truth-telling either? It's one thing, I suppose, to suggest that Christ's Sermon on the Mount contains no truths, but do you really wish your readers to accept that writers such as Chaucer, Shakespeare, Dickens, Dostoyevsky ... the entire canon of world literature ... is just so much *untruth*? Fiction?

But something has happened to you. Many years ago, three decades back in fact, you wrote your world-famous book *The Selfish Gene*, in which you established a shockingly original account of life on the planet, a new vision of what it means to be human. It was a bleak if brilliantly told story of genetically determined humanity, ultimately self-seeking: of human beings as no more than "lumbering robots" serving the interests of their gangster-like genes. And yet you redeemed that apparently unrelieved evolutionary nightmare on the very last page by appealing to the human capacity for imagination:

> We have the power to defy the selfish genes of our birth and, if necessary, the selfish memes of our indoctrination. We can even discuss ways of deliberately cultivating and nurturing pure, disinterested altruism — something that has no space in nature, something that has never existed before

in the whole history of the world. We are built as gene machines and culturally as meme machines, but we have the power to turn against our creators. We, alone on earth, can rebel against the tyranny of the selfish replicators.

Such an affirmation would accord with the intellectual and imaginative freedom of poetry, literary fiction, art; would be in accordance, too, with a measure of human liberty and moral agency. Imagination enables human beings to contemplate and model their past and their future, their origins and their destiny, their meaning and their nature: to make choices; to think scientifically and religiously too. Scientific imagination is different from religious imagination – but both find connections in at least the capacity common to both to make metaphors. But you appear in this new book to have definitively retreated from a trust in the dynamic, protean power of imagination when it comes to religion. Have you have retreated because you no longer believe in the power of the imagination to impart literary, poetic, religious, and moral truth either? Or because trust in the imagination threatens your militant atheism? Even a guardian angel cannot enter into the soul of a protégé's conscience.

4

Beauty

Let's stay with the imagination while taking a look at the section entitled "The argument from beauty". This discussion, of no more than four hundred words, tells much about your method of argument.

> I have given up counting the number of times I receive the more or less truculent "challenge": "How do you account for Shakespeare, then?" (Substitute Schubert, Michelangelo, etc. to taste.) The argument will be so familiar, I needn't document it further. But the logic behind it is never spelled

out, and the more you think about it the more vacuous you realize it to be.

Well, I'm not sure that you yourself have spelled out quite what you are trying to say. The "popular strand of argument" to which you are referring is the tendency to "prove" the existence of God by appealing to great works of art — as if God routinely takes time out of eternity to speak through artists. Is this really a popular claim? There are those who see connections between artistic creation and acknowledgment of a Creator (which I'll come to), but the "logic behind" such a view is hardly "popular" and I wonder whether it is entirely "vacuous", and seldom "spelled out".

When people invoke religion in a work of art they generally mean that a religious theme or idea has inspired the work. It seems perfectly understandable, doesn't it, that an artist should be moved by a religious story without necessarily adhering to orthodox beliefs. Could anyone doubt that Bach's *Christmas Oratorio* was inspired by the Nativity story? Or that the music of Mozart's *Requiem* was influenced by the liturgy of the Mass of the Dead? Or that Michelangelo was moved by his contemplation of the sorrowing Mother of Jesus as he sculpted the *Pieta*?

You allow that art often prompts feelings of "sublimity", but then you make this curious statement: "[Shakespeare's sonnets] ... are sublime if God is there and they are sublime if he isn't." Whose standpoint are you adopting? The poet's? The reader's? God's? Or Richard Dawkins, as an angel, surveying all three? I think you might mean that a poem can have sublimity – whether the poet *believes* in God or not. That's fair enough, except it doesn't quite fit now with the next stage of your argument. You write that it's as if readers would require that Cathy and Heathcliff really exist in order to enjoy *Wuthering Heights*!

Certain accounts in books are interesting because we believe them to be factually, as opposed to artistically, true. If you read the autobiography of Robert Graves, *Goodbye to All That*, you take it on trust that it is an accurate account of his life experiences. You would hardly enjoy the book in the same way were you to be told that he had made most of it up. Although the Gospels are not history in the modern sense, they can be read in the reasonable confidence that Jesus Christ actually lived and walked the earth 2,000 years ago; that he chose followers, preached a striking message about love, told parables, and was crucified. Accepting that Christ was the Son of God, performed miracles, rose from the dead, and ascended into heaven certainly requires something more than routine credibility: it requires faith. But is this comparable to requiring that to "enjoy" *Wuthering Heights*, a reader must believe that its characters actually existed? Surely not. A willing *suspension of disbelief* such as one adopts when reading plays, novels, and poetry is not at all the same as faith; and your insinuation that people are incapable of making such a distinction betrays a poor regard for the reading public.

Finally, you issue a challenge: "If there is a logical argument linking the existence of great art to the existence of God, it is not spelled out by its proponents. It is simply assumed to be self-evident, which it most certainly is not."

You don't seem to have looked very far. You might not agree with it, but here is one example among many of just such an argument – spelled out at length by George Steiner in an entire book, entitled *Real Presences*. He sets out his theme thus:

> That any coherent account of the capacity of human speech to communicate meaning and feeling is, in the final analysis, underwritten by the assumption of God's presence. I will put forward the argument that the experience of aesthetic meaning in particular, that of literature, of the arts, of musical form, infers the necessary possibility of this "real presence."

"Assumption" and "necessary possibility" of God's presence is not the same as "requiring that God actually exists". Steiner, an eminent literary critic, is arguing, as have others before him – William Blake, Samuel Taylor Coleridge, Matthew Arnold, T. S. Eliot, C. S. Lewis – that there is a connection, by analogy, between authentic original artistic creativity and the idea of the sustaining creation of God in the world. Steiner is not making precise claims about any particular theology, or version of revelation, or faith; and he is not offering a "proof" for the existence of God. He is talking of the sense of the createdness of the world on the horizon of an artist's consciousness, and indeed of those who appreciate art. You can be certain that while there is plenty of wood and plastic around there will be new tables; you can never be certain that another poem, or piece of music, or work of sculpture will be created. He is making, moreover, a corresponding claim: that a loss of this sense of a wager on God's presence would likely spell the degeneration and disappearance of art in our lives. It may well be that Steiner deplores the threat to art more than he would deplore a loss of the assumption of God's presence, but his argument is certainly "spelled out", and he by no means thinks it to be "self-evident".

5

What is Religion?

Let's think about the scope and meaning of the word "religion". What do people mean when they talk about religion, or the religious?

You think religion is "a persistent false belief held in the face of strong contradictory evidence". I am sure you realise that this hardly exhausts the meaning for most people, still less those who study it academically – theologians, philosophers, historians, and anthropologists. Religion, of course, is only partly involved in actual beliefs or doctrines, and these beliefs, if truly religious, are rarely held (except by fundamentalists) to be literal explanations of the world.

At the outset of your book, you insist that religion must be scientifically or empirically verifiable. And yet, for most of those who have studied religion down the ages, it is as much a product of the imagination as art, poetry, and music. Religion's activities, its rituals, its mythologies, hymns, meditations, prayers, chants, poetry, images, parables, legends, taboos, and sacramentals (by which I mean holy objects, such as candles, incense, oils, vestments, holy water) are principally symbolic, often appealing to deep levels of folk memory. Symbols might be said to be *strong* or *weak*, rather than true or false, in so far as they participate in that which they attempt to make intelligible. If I say, for example, that bread is the staff of life, I doubt whether you would claim that this is "a false belief held in the face of strong contradictory evidence". And yet you are likely to bring this claim against the ritual of Eucharistic bread, which involves a similar dynamic symbolism of real presence.

The poet Samuel Taylor Coleridge once gazed upon the fountains in Saint Peter's Square in Rome and was gripped by the force of the tangible natural metaphor, the permanence of the form, the ever-changing matter – which struck him as a living symbol of the infinite residing within the finite: and there was the fountain, its consistent shape and its permanent flow, and the image of it he carried away. Many of the symbols and rituals of religion are formalised versions of Coleridge's insight: from Easter fire to the waters of baptism, from incense to the libations of funeral rites.

It is interesting that one of the great sociologists of religion, Emile Durkheim, stated boldly in his book *The Elementary Forms of the Religious Life* that "in reality there are no religions which are false. All are true in their own fashion: all answer, albeit in different ways, to the given conditions of human existence." Much the same could be said, of course, of art. Religious rituals and symbols, from the dawning of human history, marked and celebrated birth, growth, age, death and burial, the making of families and communities, the coming together for feasts, husbandry, hunting, journeys, the life cycles of plants, animals, and human beings, the changing seasons, the diurnal, lunar, and annual rounds, the mystery of existence. The great world religions, tried and tested, as sources of flourishing over three millennia, continue to enact and celebrate those cyclical experiences and underlying mysteries. It is exciting to think of the deepening of our awareness of the world through the scientific dimension, especially cosmology and biology, and yet science cannot encompass the multi-dimensional symbols of religion, which by their nature resist explanation and control.

It might interest you, moreover, that a long tradition of philosophy sees religion as a kind of "virtue". Thomas Aquinas, the medieval church philosopher, locates this virtue in the area of justice. Justice is of course a matter of giving people or things their proper due; religion is a matter of giving God His proper due. As with all virtues (according to Aristotle, the great philosopher of ancient Greece) it is possible to fall off the tightrope of virtuous behaviour in two ways. Behaviour that fails to exhibit the virtue of religion is behaviour that either treats God as a creature, or treats a creature as God – idolatry.

It was only after the Enlightenment that the word "religion" principally came to mean an aspect of human behaviour or culture. And in the conflicts between throne and altar, Church and state, priesthood and politics, there emerged a concerted and determined effort to describe religion as a private, purely personal activity. The struggle to banish religion to the private sphere continues to this day. You would wish to see religion banished from the private sphere too.

6

Is God Supernatural?

This follows somewhat on my last! I must take you up on this word "supernatural", which you use constantly as applied to religion and God. You tell your readers that "for the vast majority of people 'religion' implies 'supernatural'". I want to sort out this word. The concept of "supernatural" was originally developed to describe behaviour that outstrips the natural capacities of any creature. As the redoubtable theologian Nicholas Lash would tell generation after generation of his students at Cambridge: "If you were to come across a rabbit playing Mozart on the violin you could bet your bottom dollar you have witnessed a supernatural phenomenon, for rabbits don't have it in them to play the violin." So when you come to think about it: this phenomenon you call God is the one being who can NOT act supernaturally, for how could God outperform His natural abilities? And yet you use the term of God routinely.

Which brings me to what you call the God hypothesis. You define God as "a superhuman, supernatural [there you go again] intelligence who deliberately designed and created the universe and everything in it, including us". This coincides with the opinion of a lot of atheistic polemicists who define God purely within the bounds of science, rather than in terms of a relationship, a quest for spiritual contact. Hence you reduce God by declaring that "any creative intelligence, of sufficient complexity to design anything, comes into existence only as the end product of an extended process of gradual evolution."

When theologians attempt to describe God's reality (His mind, say) they are all too well aware of the trap known as anthropomorphism: of treating God as a human creature. Yet it seems pointless to remind you that thousands of studies have been published on this theme down the centuries emphasising the apophatic nature of God: in other words, the impossibility of speaking about him in anything but inadequate terms. Those inadequate terms are broadly speaking metaphorical, and analogical (try dipping into James Ross's *Portraying Analogy,* or Paul Ricoeur's *The Rule of Metaphor*). And while we're on metaphors, I have to say that your consistent image of God resembles nothing so much as a megalomaniac designer-scientist. A Great Big Science Professor in the Sky.

Speaking inadequately of God, however, does not mean that religious believers never strive to articulate, and understand, as far as their intellects will carry them, even the deepest mysteries of faith. I note, however, that whenever you refer to the mystery of, for example, the Trinity – by which Christians believe that there are three persons in the one God – you get abusive: you call it a "weird thing", and you go on to write that believers "are not *meant* to understand". Finally you lecture your readers: "Don't even *try* to understand one of these, for the attempt might destroy it." You add that believers think that they "gain fulfilment in calling it a mystery". Go and sit in the reading room of the Oxford theology faculty library sometime. You might get a very weird feeling indeed when you look around and see the tiers and tiers of books dedicated to just such attempts to understand the Trinity, and a great many other mysteries besides.

And yet, you yourself, I note, are not averse to taking mysteries on faith. As you write in *Unweaving the Rainbow*: "Further developments of the [Big Bang] theory, supported by all available evidence, suggests that time itself began in this mother of all cataclysms. You probably don't understand, and I certainly don't, what it can possibly mean to say that time itself began at a particular moment. But once again that is a limitation of our minds …"

A final note on metaphor, analogy, and scripture. You cannot disguise your irritation when you contemplate the Bible. "[The Bible] is not systematically evil," you write, "but just plain weird." And theologians, you complain, "pick and choose which bits of scripture to believe, which bits to write off as symbols or allegories". Your impatience with the general untidiness of the Scriptures and the different ways in which theologians, and indeed most believers, read them betrays your neglect of even minimal enquiry into the nature of scriptural scholarship. The collection of texts known as the Bible contains a variety of different literary forms, including homily, allegory, meditation, parable, chronicle, poetry, legend, folk memory, ironic aphorisms, prophecy, prayer. And this short list does not exhaust the variety of expressions to be found throughout – from the Book of Genesis to the Book of Revelation. Scholars don't so much pick and choose which bits to believe and which bits they decide to write off: they read critically on many different levels, and from many points of view, and not with the reductive aim you have in mind. The task of reading scripture critically – a task that requires a formidable array of skills and disciplines – has gone on in every era. You might, for example, take a look at Roland Barthes's essay on structural analysis as applied to Jacob's wrestle with the Angel (near to my heart, obviously) in

Genesis 32:24–32. It reveals tellingly how new insights in literary criticism have continued to deepen human understanding of just one biblical story for a twentieth-century agnostic reader.

7

Celestial Teapots

In your section on agnosticism you cite Bertrand Russell's parable of the "celestial teapot". Here it is again in brief. If one were to claim that between Earth and Mars there is a teapot in orbit, nobody could disprove the assertion, especially if one were to claim that the teapot is too small to be seen by any telescope. Yet if one were to insist that it would be an "intolerable presumption" on the part of anyone to doubt it, this would be taken as nonsense. Russell goes on to add, however: "If the existence of such a teapot were affirmed in ancient books, taught as the sacred truth every Sunday and instilled into the minds of children at school, hesitation to believe in its existence would become a mark of eccentricity and entitle the doubter to the attentions of a psychiatrist in an enlightened age or of the Inquisition in an earlier time."

Well, it's obvious what you are up to. There should be no agnosticism about the existence of a god who is no more credible than a celestial teapot, or the Tooth Fairy, or Mother Goose, or a Flying Spaghetti Monster, especially when any of these quaint fantasies would be preferable to the Abrahamic God. And this is how you characterise that God: "An invisible man – living in the sky – who watches everything you do, every minute of every day. And the invisible man has a special list of ten things he does not want you to do. And if you do any of these ten things, he has a special place, full of fire and smoke and burning and torture and anguish, where he will send you to live and suffer and burn and choke and scream and cry forever and ever till the end of time ... But He loves you!"

I'll come around to this characterisation a bit later. But, for now, I have another parable. How might a non-religious theist or even genuine agnostic reasonably think about God? Imagine that you are sitting on a railway embankment in the open air between two tunnels. A very long train is passing by – the carriages are exiting from one tunnel and a few moments later plunging into the other, thus appearing and disappearing one after another. It is obvious that each carriage is pulling in turn the one behind it; so without ever seeing an engine (which is not being pulled), you might well calculate, using logic rather than evidence, that an infinite series of carriages could not explain the motion of those you are witnessing: in other words, the motion of each carriage is "contingent" on the motion of the one in front of it. Since everything we know in the world is subject to contingency, being caused by something else, and since an infinite series of causes does not explain the existence of the motion in the first place, then it is surely not preposterous to wonder about the source of the origin of this contingent motion, and to deduce that the origin of that motion has not itself been moved. For thousands of years this kind of argument has been employed, culminating in the conclusion that an unmoved "prime mover" might well be the explanation for a contingent world. Such an argument may not satisfy a sophisticated philosopher, nor even a scientist, but at least it has the force of reasonable speculation in contrast to Russell's arbitrary celestial teapot.

Another, equally reasonable speculation, sometimes characterised as a God of the Gaps argument, was raised by the eminent physicist Freeman Dyson in his book *Disturbing the Universe,* published in 1976, the same year as your *Selfish Gene.* Dyson, by no means a religious believer, points to the existence of some striking laws of physics constituting an array of numerical accidents that "conspire" to make the universe hospitable to life:

The strength of the attractive nuclear forces is just sufficient to overcome the electrical repulsion between the positive charges in the nuclei of ordinary atoms such as oxygen or iron. But the nuclear forces are not quite strong enough to bind together two protons (hydrogen nuclei) into a bound system which would be called a diproton if it existed. If the nuclear forces had been slightly stronger than they are, the diproton would exist and almost all the hydrogen in the universe would have been combined into diprotons and heavier nuclei. Hydrogen would be a rare element, and stars like the sun, which live for a long time, by the slow burning of hydrogen in their cores, could not exist.

Dyson goes on. If the nuclear forces had been substantially weaker than they are, hydrogen could not burn at all and there would be no heavy elements. "If, as seems likely, the evolution of life requires a star like the sun, supplying energy at a constant rate for billions of years, then the strength of nuclear forces had to lie within a rather narrow range to make life possible." And this is not all. The facts of astronomy, he points out, include other numerical accidents that worked to the advantage of the existence of life, not least the distance between stars. And the rich diversity of organic chemistry, he argues, depends on a delicate balance between electrical and quantum-mechanical forces.

"There are many other lucky accidents in atomic physics," he writes. "Without such accidents, water could not exist as a liquid, chains of carbon atoms could not form complex organic molecules, and hydrogen atoms could not form a breakable bridge between molecules." Dyson felt obliged to raise questions about how so many of these "finely tuned" conditions should have come about by pure chance, and calculated that it is a mathematical impossibility. "Being a scientist, trained in the habits of thought and language of the twentieth century rather than the eighteenth, I do not claim that the architecture of the universe proves the existence of God. I claim only that the architecture of the universe is consistent with the hypothesis that mind plays an essential role in its functioning." As the distinguished cosmologist and science expositor James Jeans once wrote: "The universe begins to look more like a great thought than a great machine." For most philosophers of religion this constitutes a theistic position.

You are of course well aware of these reflections on the numerical accidents (known as the Anthropic Principle), which you characterise as Dyson's "objection". "This objection can be answered," you tell your readers, "by the suggestion, which Martin Rees himself supports, that there are many universes, co-existing like bubbles of foam, in a 'multiverse' (or 'mega verse,' as Leonard Suskind prefers to call it). The laws and constants of any one universe, such as our observable universe, are by-laws. The multiverse as a whole has a plethora of alternative sets of by-laws." So, given an infinite series of universes, each with a different set of laws of physics and chemistry, the peculiar sets of laws necessary for hospitality to life was bound to emerge eventually. Martin Rees, you allow, is talking eminent sense on this occasion.

Answering Freeman Dyson's "objection" with this "suggestion" is hardly a compelling scientific argument; nor is the positing of "many universes, co-existing like bubbles of foam, in a 'multiverse'". In fact there are no more observable data for this "suggestion" than the positing of a miniature teapot circumnavigating the Earth.

8

God's Simplicity

In relation to my last, I'd like to come back to a central argument of yours on which you base your claim that it is "almost certain" that God does not exist. You call it the Ultimate Boeing 747 gambit, and it was originally posed by the astronomer Fred Hoyle, who said that the probability of life originating on Earth is no greater than the chance that a hurricane, sweeping through a scrap yard, would have the luck to assemble a Boeing 747. This is precisely the kind of argument employed by creationists who insist that evidence of exquisite design in everything from beetles to human beings demands an original designer.

You take this argument and turn it on its head by insisting that only the blind, bottom-up, un-designed, cumulative, non-purposive law of evolution made it possible for the varied complexity of life on the planet to emerge from the less complex. Had the process not occurred in this way, had it been the work of an originating Creator, then it would have implied that "any God", as you put it, "capable of designing anything would have to be complex enough to demand the same kind of explanation in his own right." But then, you ask, whence the designer of the ultimate designer? Does this not result in an infinite regress in order to solve the problem of an infinite regress? Hence you conclude: "Far from terminating the vicious regress, God aggravates it with a vengeance." How, you ask, do theists "cope with the argument that any God capable of designing a universe, carefully and foresightfully tuned to lead our evolution, must be a supremely complex and improbable entity who needs an even bigger explanation than the one he is supposed to provide"? And, again, you ask: "If he has the powers attributed to him he must have something far more elaborately and non-randomly constructed than the largest brain or the largest computer we know."

You are quite aware, of course, that theologians deny that God is made up of parts, or material complexity; you know that they insist on His "simplicity". And you recollect how at a Cambridge conference on science and religion you did combat with a group of them on the question. "I challenged the theologians to answer the point that a God capable of designing a universe, or anything else, would have to be complex and statistically improbable. The strongest response I heard was that I was brutally foisting a scientific epistemology upon an unwilling theology. Theologians had always defined God as simple." So it's back to your original argument: how does a simple God create mightily complex living "artefacts"? It is a patent impossibility, you aver.

Yet perhaps those Cambridge theologians misunderstood you. You were hardly "brutally foisting a scientific epistemology" on them, since your argument does not appeal to a scientific procedure in the first place. Most scientists, including yourself, hold that the history of the universe, and of evolution, has been played out within time, which begins at the Big Bang and is, philosophically speaking, an aspect of created order: contingent on the physical universe and its history. While science explores the material universe, it is only a partial description of a reality, from which consciousness, value, and purpose are missing. You take it for granted that "'God created the world' refers to an act which God performed a long time ago", just as you consider him a fact in the world, assuming him to be made up of material parts with a very big biological brain. You think of God and the universe as A + B, as if they were two entities: as if God were an object competing with other objects for our attention. But that's not at all how theologians think of God.

Perhaps the most extraordinary statement in the midst of this key chapter, though, is your indignant comment that theists have made no attempt to answer your objections on the nature of God ("what attempts," you demand, "have theists made to reply?"). Ironic that you ask this, after refusing to acknowledge that theology is a proper field of study, and having declined to embark on even a modest reading programme. This is hardly the place to make good that deficiency, but the notion that the universe proceeds from a "mind", as Dyson puts it, or a "thought", as Jeans puts it, is at least a starting point. Their descriptions stretch language to breaking point – for human beings find it hard to conceive of mind or thought in the absence of a biological brain. Yet granting, as these reasonable scientists do, the evidence of at least analogies with "mind" and "thought" as basic conditions of the universe, and granting further that these conditions are not the product of a biological brain (however large), at least gives a hint as to what God's mind and thoughts, for want of better words, might *not* be. There is also a hint here of the nature of his simplicity.

9

Theories of Everything

Coming back to the Anthropic Principle, I must comment on your optimism about the coming Theory of Everything that will finally resolve all unanswered questions about the origins of the universe. This is how you put it:

> I am optimistic that the physicists of our species will complete Einstein's dream and discover the final theory of everything before superior creatures, evolved on another world, make contact and tell us the answer ... I am optimistic that this final scientific enlightenment will deal an overdue deathblow to religion and other juvenile superstitions.

Many have looked to Professor Stephen Hawking, the mathematical physicist who in 1988 wrote in his *Brief History of Time* that he expected in his own lifetime to discover this final theory. As he put it: "Then we shall all, philosophers, scientists, and just ordinary people, be able to take part in the discussion of the question of why it is that we and the universe exist. If we find the answer to that, it would be the ultimate triumph of human reason – for then we should know the mind of God." In 2004, however, Stephen Hawking finally came round to the conclusion that the pursuit of the Theory of Everything was in vain. His decision was a result of revisiting a proof that has fascinated mathematical physicists for many decades.

It involves a great German mathematician, David Hilbert, and an Austrian logician, Kurt Gödel, who escaped Nazi Germany to settle in America at the beginning of the Second World War. The story begins in 1900 at a mathematical congress in Paris, where Hilbert set for the mathematicians of the world a list of problems for completion in the new century. Not least, he challenged them to demonstrate that mathematics is self-proving. He asked for a computational method, or algorithm, for resolving any kind of mathematical problem. Most of the leading mathematicians and logicians of the day, including Bertrand Russell, thought that this could be achieved. But in 1931 Kurt Gödel wrote a proof that upset Hilbert's proposal. He demonstrated that there are mathematical statements that no conceivable computer, however capacious, could settle.

Crucially, philosophers of science have shown that what goes for mathematics goes for physics too. Among early reactions to Hawking's announcement of his quest for a Theory of Everything, a number of peer academics had attempted to expose the Gödel flaw in Hawking's proposal. Gödel had shown, they insisted, that in principle and for all time a Theory of Everything was bound to be either incomplete or inconsistent. These included world-class mathematicians and theoretical physicists such as Roger Penrose of Oxford (author of *The Emperor's New Mind*), Paul Davies, then of Newcastle (author of *The Mind of God*), and the then professor of mathematics at Sussex University, John Barrow (author of *Impossibility*). "What Gödel shows," said Barrow, who now holds the chair in public understanding of mathematics in Cambridge, "is that no final theory of everything is possible; and that in any case there could be no algorithm, or mechanical procedure, that enables you to prove such a theory." But their earlier objections had been drowned out in the enthusiastic hype that surrounded Hawking's book.

Sixteen years after its publication Hawking returned to Gödel and, on pondering its implications, published a paper titled "Gödel and the End of Physics". "Gödel's theorem," he explains, "is proved using statements that refer to themselves. Such statements can lead to paradoxes. An example is, this statement is false. If the statement is true, it is false; and if the statement is false, it is true."

The connection between Gödel's theorem and the impossibility of a Theory of Everything is "obvious", he adds:

> ... if there are mathematical results that cannot be proved, there are physical problems that cannot be predicted ... we are not angels who view the universe from the outside. Instead, we and our models, are both part of the universe we are describing. Thus a physical theory, is self-referencing, like in Gödel's theorem. One might therefore expect it to be either inconsistent, or incomplete.

He has commented on this volte-face:

> Some people will be very disappointed ... but I have changed my mind. I'm now glad that our search for understanding will never come to an end, and that we will always have the challenge of new discovery. Without it, we would stagnate. Gödel's theorem ensured there would always be a job for mathematicians.

That is the remarkable result of Hawking's re-reading of Gödel's proof. *A Brief History of Time* announced to an entire generation that the universe was both describable and explicable in terms of a single theory in physics. By implication, however, it down-graded all other forms of intellectual endeavour, including philosophy, theology, anthropology, literature, history. It signalled the final triumph of science as the ultimate explicator. Your book, of course, goes one stage further: a Theory of Everything would signal, for you, the final fall of God and religion.

The Hawking renunciation shows the danger of pinning too much on these physicists and their dreams of a final theory. In the meantime perhaps you too should pay a pilgrimage to Gödel's theorem.

10

Dawkins versus Dostoyevsky

There can be very few people alive today who would boast ethical superiority over the novelist Fyodor Dostoyevsky. You depict the powerful character of the young man Ivan Karamazov, in Dostoyevsky's *The Brothers Karamazov*, as believing that if God does not exist then everything is permitted. In other words, a world without belief in God is bound to be a world of unbridled crime and sin. It does of course appear rather a crass viewpoint; and it surely seems odd that Dostoyevsky, as you claim, shared in that crassness.

> It seems to me to require quite a low self-regard to think
> that, should belief in God suddenly vanish from the world,
> we would all become callous and selfish hedonists, with
> no kindness, no charity, no generosity, nothing that would
> deserve the name of goodness. It is widely believed that
> Dostoevsky was of that opinion ...

You are happy to inform your readers, with the neat disclaimer
– "[p]erhaps naively" – that you have inclined towards a less
cynical view of human nature than Dostoyevsky. "Do we really
need policing – whether by God or by each other – in order to
stop us from behaving in a selfish and criminal manner? I dearly
want to believe that I do not need such surveillance – and nor,
dear reader, do you."

There seems to be a misunderstanding between you and the
great novelist, perhaps as a result of your misreading of his
work; perhaps as a result of your contrasting backgrounds and
experience of life. You have never spent time in a prison. You
moved in smooth transition through prep school, to private secondary school and on to Oxford, where you have been mostly
resident through your working life, and where you have formed
your mainly optimistic view of the world.

Dostoyevsky began writing *The Brothers Karamazov* in 1878,
aged fifty-seven. As a child he had suffered the loss of both
parents (it is believed that his father was murdered) and in his

thirties he spent five years in prison, including several months on death row and four years as a convict in a labour camp. He was an epileptic, a state of mental health not helped by being subjected to a mock execution, facing a firing squad from which he was reprieved at the last moment. His crime was to have been a member of a liberal underground society.

Dostoyevsky had first-hand knowledge of much tragedy and suffering: a Russian mid-nineteenth-century labour camp, overcrowded, lacking food and in hygiene, and infested with lice and disease. In his forties he tried to make sense of all that darkness and violence in the light of influential ideas from the West. These included the English Utilitarianism of Bentham and Stuart Mill, Utopian Marxism, and a set of ideas that you would have applauded – Social Darwinism. Dostoyevsky also struggled to understand how Christianity could withstand the new Russian Nihilism (which rejected all forms of religion, morality, and politics). The conflicts and tensions between these competing ideologies and religion are of course dramatised at length in his great novels. So we come to the character of Ivan Karamazov, a convinced atheist, who voices many of the intellectual scruples that assailed Dostoyevsky, but hardly paralleled his entire thinking. While Ivan is acquainted with arguments for and against the existence of God, his atheism has less to do with science, reasoned proofs, and philosophy than his consciousness of the "human tears with which the earth is saturated from its crust to its centre". He retains a zest for life despite its patent cruelty and absurdity, but he is convinced, through personal experience, that human existence is ultimately meaningless: that there is no God. He has become aloof, isolated, self-reliant, and egoistic, extremely judgmental of his fellow human beings; judgmental of every image and suggestion of a God.

In opposition to Ivan there is the saintly monk, Father Zosima, who teaches through the example of Jesus Christ that one must love non-judgmentally, unconditionally, and universally as well as particularly. The meaning of life for Father Zosima is to be found in the rejection of egoism. Ivan's younger brother Alyosha, who has been a monastic novice, speaks for Father Zosima's teaching while Ivan explains the reasons for his atheism.

Ivan does not indict God for natural disasters in the world – disease, earthquakes, and so forth – since he can accept, in theory, that these trials, should God exist, might have a divine purpose – to purge and to test the human race. What Ivan cannot stomach is a God who has given adult humans the freedom to inflict suffering on children. Ivan is not so much saying: take away God and everything is permitted; he is saying that he *knows* that God does not exist, and that is *why* everything is permitted.

To demonstrate this awful circumstance, Ivan tells his

brother Alyosha that he has made a collection of atrocities, "certain interesting little facts ... from newspapers and books ... certain jolly little anecdotes," as Ivan puts it with heavy irony. These are cuttings taken from true newspaper accounts, although hardly the stuff of the *Oxford Mail*: soldiers who sliced babies from their mother's wombs and impaled them on their bayonets; a father and a mother who stuffed faeces in the mouth of their five-year-old daughter and locked her in an outside freezing lavatory all night for having wet the bed; a Russian general who ordered his hounds to tear to pieces an eight-year-old boy because he had accidentally wounded the paw of one of his dogs.

For Ivan there is no possible religious argument, including hell for the perpetrators, that would justify a God who permits such savagery against children. "It is not worth one little tear of that tortured little girl who beat herself on the breast and prayed to her 'dear, kind Lord' in the stinking privy with her unexpiated tears." Any attempt, Ivan goes on, to justify God's creation of this freedom to abuse is an insult to these innocent victims.

Dostoyevsky's response comes not in the form of a counter-argument but enacted in the life of his brother Alyosha through to the end of the narrative. Unlike Ivan, who boasts that he possesses a Euclidian mind – a Westernised scientific and mathematical mind – Alyosha has become practised in a Russian

Orthodox spirituality, open to the influence of God in the world. For him the Euclidean parallel lines of the spiritual and material, deemed separate into infinity, meet and intertwine. This kind of spirituality is not amenable, obviously, to empirical proof, nor even to rational argument, but to a sense of God's presence in the world exemplified in the mysticism of the Orthodox icon. The icon, crafted to the sound of prayer, is not so much a representation of the spiritual realm as a manifestation of real divine presence radiating out, and penetrating, the world: it looks *out*, rather than is looked *at*.

After Father Zosima dies, Alyosha becomes transfigured by a sense of God's radiating presence, which comes in the form of a gift rather than by his own spiritual striving or attainment. All that is necessary is openness to the gift. "The silence of the earth seemed to merge with the silence of the heavens, the mystery of the earth to be touched by the mystery of the stars ... It was as if threads from all those innumerable worlds of God all came together in his soul." In consequence Alyosha experiences an overpowering inclination to non-judgmental, communal love.

Dostoyevsky proclaims, through Zosima and Alyosha, that Christ's divine self-emptying is the ultimate exemplar of selfless love. Zosima has taught Ivan's brother how to become not an I but a Thou: one that exists in self-giving for others, one who learns to feel and to love communally, rather than one trapped in isolated, self-willed egoism. Alyosha, as the novel progresses, does not collect stories of children's sufferings; he seeks to find actual suffering children, and to identify with them in practice, coping with the problem of evil and suffering in action rather than arguments.

Dostoyevsky's intention by the end of the novel is to reveal Alyosha as an icon of Christ. But Alyosha vociferously resists any praise for his deeds. Only Christ, he responds, is deserving of worship since he is the only human being who has suffered and lost everything for the sake of others. Hence only Christ can forgive everything – even those who have tortured and murdered children.

I go to these lengths not in any expectation that you will be convinced by these accounts, but to impress upon you the contrast between your version of Dostoyevsky on morality, and an alternative reading – which, even so, hardly exhausts the complexities of meaning contained in that great novel.

I I

Jesus, the Jews, and the "Pigs"

At the heart of your book is an attempt to deny the origins
of the Christian message of universal love, or *agape* (un-
conditional love of all), by claiming that Jesus, like his Jewish
predecessors, counselled altruism only within the Jewish in-
group: outsiders, aliens, foreigners, as far as Jesus was concerned, counted for nothing. This view is of course a striking
reversal of historical accounts of Christ's message, as related
in the New Testament. You make no claims to having studied
the appropriate biblical texts other than to have acquainted
yourself with a specific source, which you recommend to your
readers.

This is an article entitled "Love Thy Neighbour: the Evolution of In-Group Morality", by John Hartung (originally published in *Skeptic*, Vol. 3, No. 4, 1995, also available on a website known as Stalking the Wild Taboo: www.lrainc.com/swtaboo). A medical doctor, and part-time social anthropologist, Hartung was an associate professor of anaesthesiology at the State University of New York at the time of writing his article. Given that the article deviates strikingly from the accepted accounts of Christian teaching on love, and given that Professor Hartung has no pretensions to being a scriptural scholar, I wondered about your dependence on this single source. Would you, for example, accept a similar circumstance within your own subject, biology? If you had set an essay on, say, the independent evolution of eyes, and a student had turned in an essay based on a single source, claiming that the theory of the independent evolution of eyes was wrong, would you not be astonished? Would you not send the student back to the library to make a wider survey of the literature?

Whatever the case, you begin your endorsement of Hartung's views as follows:

> I need to call attention to one particularly unpalatable
> aspect of [the Bible's] ethical teaching. Christians seldom
> realize that much of the moral consideration for others
> which is apparently promoted by both the Old and New

Testaments was originally intended to apply only to a narrowly defined in-group. "Love thy neighbour" didn't mean what we now think it means. It meant only "Love another Jew."

The text invoked by Hartung is Leviticus 19:18. In the Revised Standard Version, it is translated: "You shall not take vengeance or bear a grudge against any of your people, but you shall love your neighbour as yourself." In this context, argues Hartung, with your endorsement, neighbour means "fellow in-group members". From which you both deduce that the Ten Commandments, prohibiting murder, adultery, theft, false witness, and so forth, apply only to other Jews.

There is, however, a straightforward lesson to be derived from Leviticus 19:18 that may not have occurred to you: that loving one's neighbours can be very hard indeed, more hard perhaps than loving a stranger, and that such an ideal needs to be strived for. But, following Hartung, you argue that the instruction to regard only Jews as neighbours is an absolute, hence ignoring the counsel given a few verses further on: "When an alien resides within you in your land, you shall not oppress the alien … You shall love the alien as yourself." It seems to me odd that you consistently accuse believers of picking and choosing the texts that suit them, and yet you do not scruple to do the same yourself in order to paint Judaism in a bad light.

Moving on to Hartung's treatment of the same issue in the New Testament, you write: "Hartung puts it more bluntly than I dare: 'Jesus would have turned over in his grave if he had known that Paul would be taking his plan to the pigs." Hartung is saying that it was Paul who claimed that the Messiah had come to save all peoples and not just Jews, whereas Jesus would have referred to, and regarded, non-Jews as pigs – the Goyim being pig-eaters.

Again, you have ignored the reflection made by Jesus himself on the subject of the Leviticus 19:18 text. It is of course the famous parable of the Good Samaritan. An expert in Jewish religious law asks Jesus what he must do to earn eternal life. Jesus responds by asking the lawyer what Mosaic law says on the subject, and the man responds: "Love God with all your heart, with all your soul, with all your strength and all your mind." Then he adds the admonition as in Leviticus 19:18: "Love your neighbour as yourself." Jesus' answer – "Do this and you will live" – can be taken to mean that those who follow this commandment, whether they are Jews or not, will inherit eternal life. The lawyer then asks Jesus: "And who is my neighbour?" Whereupon Jesus tells him the story of the traveller who has been robbed and lies dying by the roadside. First a priest, wishing to avoid ritual purity, passes; then a Levite, a scholar of Jewish law, does the same. Finally a Samaritan comes along, a person regarded as heretical and unclean. He stops to adminis-

ter first aid, and brings the wounded man to an inn, promising
to cover any expenses.

Jesus asks the lawyer to judge who was the victim's neighbour. Unwilling even to utter the word "Samaritan", he replies:
"The one who helped him." Jesus says: "Go and do the same."
The message of Christianity, then, is not about legal obligation,
but the obligation to exercise compassion, respect, and love,
irrespective of race or creed. As the scriptural scholar John J.
Kilgallen points out in his *Brief Commentary on the Gospel of Luke*
(1988), the meaning of the story is also aimed at those repre-
sented by the Good Samaritan. For Samaritans were similarly
taught to despise Jews. In a modern rendering of the story, a
Palestinian giving aid to a Jew might provide a suitable parallel.
It is also worth noting, in response to you and Hartung, that
the dialogue shows that the definition of "neighbour" was a
topic of controversy during Jesus' lifetime, a controversy that
the parable conclusively settles for those who would be followers of Jesus.

But Hartung's background thesis about Judaism deserves
closer attention. Here it is in his own words, as quoted in full
in your *God Delusion*:

> The Bible is a blueprint of in-group morality, complete
> with instructions for genocide, enslavement of out-groups,
> and world domination. But the Bible is not evil by virtue

of its objectives or even its glorification of murder, cruelty, and rape. Many ancient works do that — The Iliad, the Icelandic sagas … but no one is selling the Iliad as a foundation for morality. Therein lies the problem. The Bible is sold, and bought, as a guide to how people should live their lives. And it is, by far, the world's all-time best seller.

The charge is that the Bible teaches doctrines of genocide, enslavement and world domination. Christianity, referred to by Hartung in the article (so much praised by you) as "Judaism's recusant evangelical sect", is of course thus deemed to be influenced by the same "in-group morality". But there is a deeper significance in this thesis, more clearly expressed in a warm review published by Hartung in 1995 of a book entitled *A People That Shall Dwell Alone: Judaism as a Group Evolutionary Strategy*, by Professor Kevin MacDonald (the review was originally published in the July issue of *Ethology and Sociobiology* and also appears on the website Stalking the Wild Taboo). MacDonald, an American psychologist (and expert witness for David Irving in his libel action against Deborah Lipstadt in 2000), was arguing, according to Hartung, "that the worldwide, age-old phenomenon of anti-semitism is not a disease state vectored by myths, but is instead what should be expected given the nature of human intergroup competition and the competitive attributes of Judaism".

Hartung is at pains in this review to endorse the notion that anti-Semitism does not originate in routine racism, but in something he terms "reactive racism" — meaning an understandable racial response to the determined genocidal doctrines of the Jews. "History is replete," writes Hartung, "with the consequences of that form of reactive racism which we call anti-Semitism, and MacDonald is in the vanguard of those who will broaden our understanding of its origins." The pay-off of the Hartung–MacDonald thesis is as follows:

> The modern state of Israel receives the monetary equivalent of more than 625,000 pounds of gold per year, primarily from the United States. Isaiah's dream has come true and it rests on two pillars:
>
> (1) most of the citizens of most donor nations are Christian or Jewish, such that, the former religion being a form of the latter, to varying degrees they believe in a god who gave Palestine to the Jews, and
>
> (2) the most enormous act of reactive racism ever perpetrated, namely the Holocaust, has been presented, and so is perceived, as having been the psychotic swelling up of a form of evil that resides disproportionately in the souls of Goyim — and so they have been induced to irrationally atone for their special evil by enabling descendant and non descendant coreligionists of the

Jewish victims of the Holocaust to systematically purloin the land and property of people who were not those victims' persecutors. MacDonald's work will help us chip away at this second pillar and that makes it very good work indeed.

In view of the controversial nature of Hartung's views, including his espousal of MacDonald, whose background and theories can be ascertained from a number of internet sources, I find it strange that you should have been so reliant on this single source for what forms such an important charge against Judaism and Christianity in your book.

12

Dawkins's Utopia

I want to write to you now about your Utopia. You have issued a glowing promise of ultimate happiness, if only your readers will trust in you. You want them to believe in a paradise that will be theirs when religion is finally wiped from the face of the Earth. You sing to them a version of John Lennon's famous song "Imagine".

"Imagine ... a world with no religion. Imagine no suicide bombers, no 9/11, no 7/7, no Crusades, no witch-hunts ... no Israeli/Palestinian wars, no Serb/Croat/Muslim massacres, no persecution of Jews as 'Christ-killers', no Northern Ireland 'troubles' ... no Taliban to blow up ancient statues".

Your list has quite a ring to it (although some of your instances might well have been the result of secular tensions), but it omits two catastrophic eras in recent history: Stalin's Soviet Union and Hitler's Germany. Should we be concerned that Stalinism and Nazism revealed the kind of world that emerges when religion acquiesces not to just anything, but to science as ideology combined with militant atheism?

You do intend, don't you, to replace religion with science. "If the demise of God will leave a gap," you tell your readers, "... My way includes a good dose of science, the honest and systematic endeavour to find out the truth about the real world." Do I detect an echo of Christ's words: "I am the Way, the Truth, and the Light"?

Science of course has delivered the great benefits to humankind: myriad therapies for disease and suffering, greater food security, speedy means of travel, wealth, better housing, communications, entertainment, physical comfort. Even the promise, as you have put it, of a "totally satisfying naturalistic explanation for the existence of the Universe and everything that's in it including ourselves".

Should we not be concerned though that triumphalist science allied itself through the last century with totalitarianism? Should we not worry just a little that science has underpinned political philosophies aimed at enslaving humankind, rather than promoting freedom? Should we be anxious about the technologies science has spawned, polluting the planet to the point of threatening its very survival? And what of weapons of mass destruction? As for explanations, there are those whose materialist, determinist "scientistic" philosophies have argued for the deconstruction of the human person and freedom of the will. Should we not be concerned about all this in a world based on science and militant atheism? I know that scientists did not drop those bombs on Hiroshima and Nagasaki; but they were involved in their making, just as scientists have been responsible for researching and constructing such weapons ever since.

It is well known that Stalin's brand of Communism found its origin in an idea called dialectical materialism – a self-proclaimed scientific and atheistic ideology. Marx, moreover, characterised religion as the "opium of the people", conjuring up a dream of the perfectibility of humankind according to mechanical laws that operate like those of the natural sciences. Friedrich Engels said of Marx at his funeral: "Just as Darwin had discovered the law of development of organic nature so did Marx discover the law of human history." And this law of human history became in time the basis of a dictatorship, for its tenets did not admit of doubt or diversity of values and opinions. I only raise these matters as others will most certainly produce them, boringly perhaps, as palpable objections to your Utopia.

Your opponents, moreover, are liable to object that Marxist-

Leninism provided a powerful impetus for murderous purges of political dissidents and religious believers alike. Under Stalin, they will argue, Russia saw the devastating implementation of socio-biological principles based on Lamarck – the inheritance of acquired characteristics – legitimizing strategies of enforced collectivisation of agricultural labour, and ruinous systems of agricultural production.

And what of Hitler? Not much of a scientist, the Führer, but his appeal to bio-politics, to the science of racial hered-ity, evoked images of Jews as parasitical invasions of the host body of German-hood. Jews were responsible, Nazi propaganda claimed, for actual epidemics in the East requiring immediate quarantine – early euphemisms for the ghettos and the camps. In the pathological paradox that attends science as salvation, the purveyors of death paraded their cynical pretensions to preserve human life. I was reminded of this when reading your characterisation of religion as a kind of cultural virus, a clever idea of yours which you call a "meme". I could not help noting that some of your most ardent followers have already charac-terised religion as a sort of viral infection, an HIV of the mind, requiring drastic final solutions – quarantine, liquidation.

Have you read the *Table Talk* ramblings of Hitler on reli-gion's capitulation to science? Just listen to him! "The dogma of Christianity gets worn away before the advances of science. Religion will have to make more and more concessions. Gradually the myths crumble. When understanding of the universe has become widespread ... then the Christian doctrine will be convicted of absurdity."

But then, as you would I'm sure be quick to point out, Marxist-Leninism, Stalinism, and National Socialism appealed not to good science but to bad science. Scientific theories are of course, all of them, provisional, falsifiable, subject to advances, retreats, and transformations. Newtonian atomism, like Newtonian cosmology, made its contribution and passed into the history of science as a paradigm lost, yet nobody would wish to describe Newtonian physics as pseudo-science. In any case we rely on scientists such as yourself, Richard, to inform us as to what is authentic science and what is pseudo-science. I see that you are not inclined to grant such a distinction to religion; but then that would likely weaken your overall scheme.

You are nevertheless concerned about your readers' attitude towards Hitler and Stalin, as purveyors of atheism as an ideology. You argue that they were merely unfortunate by-products, the necessary "sawtooth" of history, you call it, a mere bit of rough with the smooth, as science and encroaching atheism escort the human race ever onwards and upwards.

You are evidently ruffled by suggestions that Hitler is a monstrous exception. "Hitler's ideas and intentions were not self-evidently more evil than those of Caligula – or some of the Ottoman sultans," you tell your readers. It worried me for a moment that this was an attempt at moral equivalence that wobbled on the brink of some kind of mitigation.

I was also intrigued by the logic of your claim that the militant atheism of Hitler and Stalin was by definition innocuous. "Hitler and Stalin shared atheism in common," you write, "they both also had moustaches, as does Saddam Hussein. So what?"

Would a critic not object that the atheism of Stalin and Hitler was not a private foible, like a moustache, but a public policy foisted on their people? Hitler played fast and loose with religion. Whenever and wherever he deemed religion a threat to his regime he persecuted believers and purged them. Stalin's atheism, moreover, was a crucial feature of his entire ideology. He oppressed, imprisoned, and murdered the Orthodox faithful, destroying their icons and their churches throughout the length and breadth of Russia. Mao Tse Tung, another enthusiastic atheist, followed suit, and his anti-religious policies continue to this day.

By raising Nazism and Stalinism in this way I am reminding you that the record for combined science and atheism as ideology is not good. I would agree, however, that neither science nor atheism *necessarily* leads to violence. But is it not possible that the same can be said for religion? Religion does not necessarily lead to evil. Human wickedness, persecutions, massacres, torture, ethnic cleansing arise from a complexity of human motivations – fear, insecurity, idealism, paranoia – in a mix of political, social, ideological, scientific, and yes, at times religious contexts. When religion appears to be a factor in conflicts – take Ireland, or the Balkans, or the Arab–Israeli conflict – it may be just one marker of difference, in association with others, reinforcing a variety of tensions that in turn represent a wider ambit of antagonisms – geographical, historical, tribal. But I can quite see that to accept this point would not suit your thesis.

13

Fundamentalism

I have a crucial point to make. Following on my last, I want to raise the question of fundamentalism. It's a tricky concept. In fact, I know a historian who spent ten years attempting to write a book on the subject and failed by his own admission to capture it in the round. There are those who interpret fundamentalism as a slavish, literal reading of a religious text – such as (following Genesis) believing that Almighty God created the world in six days. You write, for example, that fundamentalists "know they are right because they have read the truth in a holy book and they know, in advance, that nothing will budge them from their belief". Well, I trust that nobody would think they were right merely on the basis of reading *your* book, although I have noted on the dust-jacket the following encomium by the novelist Philip Pullman: "It should have a place in every school library — especially in the library of every 'faith' school." I suppose it's possible to write a book that replaces the Bible without a simple transference of fundamentalist leanings.

Anyway, rivers of ink have been spilt on this word "fundamentalism", which can mean a great many things.

I offer the following reflection more as a discussion point than a polemic. Ever since the period widely known as the Enlightenment, thinkers have discussed how "good societies" are formed. It has emerged in the formation of modern nation states, and I'm thinking in particular of Europe and America, that there are two principal paths available. One is to allow individuals and groups of individuals to choose their own beliefs and values freely (obviously within the framework of law); the other is to insist that beliefs and values should be enforced on everybody top-down. The former might be described as a pluralist or democratic society, in which people respect those whose views differ from their own; but the latter, the top-down imposition of values, describes a totalitarian or a *fundamentalist* one that does not allow for disagreement. So a fundamentalist might describe someone who rejects pluralism of viewpoints, values, creeds, religions, and indeed shades of doubt, scepticism, agnosticism, and atheism. Fundamentalists are swift to denounce pluralism as relativism, the idea that any belief is as good, or as bad, as any other. Fundamentalists are determined, aggressive dogmatists, insisting that they, and they alone, are right: you are either with them or against them. Do you think that it is just as possible to be a scientific fundamentalist as a religious one? I raise this as I note that you denounce all those critics who are "infected", as you put it, "with cultural relativism". But I imagine that you would hotly deny that any such construction could be placed on your thesis.

All the same, you are insistent that all religious believers are by definition fundamentalists and that even the mildest, most tolerant form of faith leads inexorably to the suicide bomber. I'm not sure that I follow you in this very radical statement. Do you mean to say that there is no difference between levels of faith? I am thinking, for example, of the Catholic writer Graham Greene, who talked of his faith as a kind of "doubt of my doubt". And I am thinking of people like yourself who hold their beliefs with exemplary certitude. You appear to have never encountered the wavering shades of scepticism experienced by most religious believers.

I suppose it's possible that belief in some souls is like an on–off switch – all or nothing – rather than a dimmer-switch constantly expanding and contracting, sometimes shading into total darkness. Take the young nineteenth-century Carmelite saint Thérèse of Lisieux, who routinely contemplated thoughts of profound nihilism:

> You might imagine [she wrote to her sister] that my soul was as full of consolations as it could hold: that for me, the veil which hides the unseen scarcely existed. And all the time it isn't just a veil, it's a great wall which reaches up to the sky and blots out the stars! ... Sometimes, it's true, a tiny ray of light pierces through the darkness, and then, just for a moment, the ordeal is over; but immediately afterward the memory of it brings me no happiness, it seems to make the darkness thicker than ever.

Faith in most people is more like a life journey, with a great many crises, interludes, and digressions than a single, final, irrevocable step; and it is rarely taken alone, or lacking influence from family, education, lovers, books, films, theatre, and the impact of poverty, wealth, health, sickness, birth, death, war, and peace.

But it's in the context of the two paths to the good society, pluralism or fundamentalism – sometimes known as totalitarianism – that you produce an argument that is unfamiliar to me. You claim, for example, that the founding fathers of America attempted to weaken the hold of religious belief on society. I am surprised at this contention. It seems to me, reading its text, that the genius of the Declaration of Independence of the United States of America, made in July 1776 under the explicit auspices of God, was its insistence on a state of governmental absence of religion, or secularism, in order to guarantee religious freedoms, including atheism, in a free and pluralist society. Are you saying that human flourishing in the American system owed nothing to the encouragement of diversity and everything to the encouragement of atheism?

I think that it is important to get this right since there are those, including sincere religious believers, who consider that the conservation of the historic American experiment could not be more urgent than today. Which brings me to the issue of respect which, you say, religion does not deserve.

The question is not whether you respect the *content* of people's faith; it is whether you respect their *right* to adopt freely chosen beliefs, within the law, without insult and persecution. There is no more powerful notional incentive for universal respect, even for agnostics, than the proposition, however assailed by scepticism, that all without exception are special: or, as I of course would prefer to put it, children of God.

Should we respect religion to the extent of banning anti-religious publications, films, and cartoons? There are times when a fine line exists between persecution and satire, especially when a powerful majority makes mockery of all that is held sacred by an insecure, hard-pressed minority. Remember how respect for the Jews was eroded through many decades in Europe, desensitising people to the return of anti-Semitism in the twentieth century.

So how far should we encourage respect? Which brings me to the debate over creationism, on which you wax heatedly. To adopt such beliefs into the science curricula of schools would of course be a gross category error. Theology is theology, and science is science, as Father Mendel would have agreed. But you yourself consistently make a striking category error by confusing creationism and the "doctrine of creation" held by many faiths. The matter is straightforward: biblical creationists believe that the Book of Genesis is a source of factual information about the origins of the world. They teach that God literally created all things in a series of instantaneous acts over six days some 5,000 years ago. Most sensible believers in the Book subscribe without demur to Darwin's theory of evolution, while reading Genesis in the light of the mystery so well articulated by Martin Rees – "Why is there something rather than nothing?" Which I shall come back to by and by.

14

Is Religious Education Child Abuse?

Here you are again in typical anecdotal mood about yourself:

Once, in the question time after a lecture in Dublin, I was asked what I thought about the widely publicized cases of sexual abuse by Catholic priests in Ireland. I replied that, horrible as sexual abuse no doubt was, the damage was arguably less than the long-term psychological damage inflicted by bringing the child up Catholic in the first place. It was an off-the-cuff remark made in the heat of the moment, and I was surprised that it earned a round of enthusiastic applause from that Irish audience (composed, admittedly, of Dublin intellectuals and presumably not representative of the country at large).

You should not be carried away by the effect of your own charisma and eloquence. A Dublin audience will clap enthusiastically in an effort to bring the most delightful evening to an end so as to make it to the bar before closing time. And I think, as a scientist, you would be the first to admit that applause neither proves, nor disproves, a proposition.

Would you really *trade* child sexual abuse for being brought up in the religion of your parents? To be fair to your own question, one would wish to investigate the worst aspects as well as the best of religious education in order to reach a judgment; whereas surely nobody who has suffered sexual abuse in childhood (or whose child has been so abused) could suggest that the experience has its redeeming features. There are patently perceived advantages to receiving a religious education, which is why people continue to make great sacrifices to defend the practice. That there are possible downsides is obvious, especially in a country like Ireland that was for generations dominated by authoritarian priests, brothers, and nuns. Oh yes, I've seen Brother Brendan thumping the daylights out of Tommy Coyne, for no good reason, while declaiming: "You're after asking yourself why Brother is givin' you the beatin'; but if you look into your heart of hearts, Tommy, you *know* that you deserved it!"

You begin making your case with anecdotes about people, educated religiously in childhood, who have suffered grievously from coming out as "atheists" on achieving adulthood. A typical email letter from a young man shares a romantic dilemma: his girlfriend has told him: "'She can't trust me ... because my morals don't come from God ...'" You wrote back: "pointing out to him that, while his girlfriend had discovered something about him, he too had discovered something about her. Was she really good enough for him? I doubted it."

You're obviously rather good at this agony uncle stuff, but I don't see how it advances a serious case for banning religious education in childhood. The circumstance might just as well have been reversed: as when an atheist couple run into difficulties after one of them decides to take up religion. I could imagine an agony uncle, of no religion, writing to the converted partner in precisely the same vein as yourself. Remember: "Love's not love that alters when it alteration finds ..."

But it takes the introduction of your friend the psychologist Nicholas Humphrey to put a bit of weighty thinking into your thesis. Humphrey was invited (not so long ago) to give a lecture sponsored by Amnesty International, and he used the occasion as an opportunity to air his views on religious education as child abuse. The fact that Amnesty normally concerns itself with prisoners of conscience is presumably a measure of the seriousness with which Dr Humphrey takes himself on this issue. So let's unpack it a bit.

Conscious that Amnesty's *raison d'être* is defence of freedom of speech, Humphrey declared that he was in favour of censorship when it came to the moral and religious education of children, especially at home "where parents are allowed – even expected – to determine for their children what counts as truth and falsehood, right and wrong". Here is Dr Humphrey:

> Children … have a human right not to have their minds crippled by exposure to other people's bad ideas – no matter who these other people are. Parents, correspondingly, have no God-given licence to enculturate their children in whatever ways they personally choose: no right to limit the horizons of their children's knowledge, to bring them up in an atmosphere of dogma and superstition, or to insist they follow the straight and narrow paths of their own faith.

I suspect that children are more in danger of being passive recipients of pompous self-righteousness than they are of religious training. But what on earth constitutes a bad idea? And who decides? And what is to be done if the advocacy is not to be just so much hot air? Humphrey initially gives two concrete instances: one is believing the literal truth of the Bible; the other is believing in astrology. I feel that the first instance is perhaps more a problem than the second – which for the majority of astrological devotees is a fairly harmless pastime. Give even young children credit for distinguishing fantasy from fact. But most fundamentalists (of the literal reading of scripture kind) would insist that their pedagogy is a "good idea" and not a bad one. So again, who is it that will sit in judgment? Presumably non-fundamentalists: but as far as you are concerned, all religionists are fundamentalists. So does this mean that only atheists will be allowed to decide when an idea is bad? And does this mean that atheists never peddle bad ideas?

Dr Humphrey, I suspect, is well aware of these objections, and is unfazed by them because his true target resides in the realms of the general rather than the particular. He proclaims that he would ban the education of children in an "atmosphere" of dogma. Well, even if parents were unerringly capable of deciding what constitutes dogma, who is to judge where an "atmosphere" starts and finishes? At the same time, he would forbid "enculturation" of children "in whatever ways" parents "personally choose". What on earth does enculturation *not* cover in the bringing up of children – sports, movies, music, books, food, toys, clothes, holiday destinations, membership of the scouts, ballet? Learning to read and write?

Your own gloss on the above indicates you were assailed by

a reasonable doubt about the Humphrey lecture: "Of course, such a strong statement needs, and received, much qualification." But then you are back to personal anecdote. "I thank my own parents for taking the view that children should be taught not so much *what* to think as *how* to think." Do you really think that children can be taught without imparting *something*? Some "what"? What did your parents do? Launch you straight into symbolic logic? "No A's are B's and some A's are C's; therefore some C's are not B's." I note, of course, that you were such a prodigy that your mother kept a notebook of your sayings (as you tell your readers on page 349). And to this day you are much taken with your own extraordinary "actings-out" in childhood. Not content with imagining yourself as such routine personifications as a "Babylonian", or an "accelerator", you indulged your fantasy, as a child, with what you termed "second-order pretendings", for example, "an owl pretending to be a waterwheel ... which might be reflexive ... now I'm a little boy pretending to be Richard". I have an impression of the grown-ups in your life gathering around you as if attending a shrine.

I must say that most sensible parents neither teach their children what to think, nor how to think, but how to *behave*. I'm an old-fashioned angel.

But you are not yet done with Dr Humphrey, who has saved his *pièce de résistance* till last. "Humphrey suggests," you venture, "that as long as children are young, vulnerable and in need of protection, truly moral guardianship shows itself in an honest attempt to second-guess what they *would* choose for themselves if they were old enough to do so." I should have thought that the last thing anybody wanted for themselves, in adulthood, was what a truly moral parent thought they *might* choose for themselves: brain surgeon, concert pianist, banker, goalie for West Ham … Is not the path of human happiness paved with rebellions against early parental ambitions and wishes? And what has choosing a role in life necessarily got to do with good or bad *ideas*?

But at this point Dr Humphrey entirely loses your plot for you. He now cites a programme "shown on American television" featuring the story of a young Inca girl whose 500-year-old remains were found frozen in the mountains of Peru in 1995. The anthropologist who discovered her maintained that she had been the victim of a ritual sacrifice.

This programme – we are not told what channel or network – apparently invited viewers to "'marvel at the spiritual commitment of the Inca priests and to share with the girl on her last journey her pride and excitement at having been selected for the signal honour of being sacrificed'". According to the shocked Dr Humphrey this dastardly programme was claiming that "'human sacrifice was in its own way a glorious cultural invention – another jewel in the crown of multiculturalism'".

"Humphrey," you expostulate, "is scandalized, and so am I ... 'how dare anyone even suggest this? How dare they invite us – in our sitting rooms, watching television – to feel uplifted by contemplating an act of ritual murder: the murder of a dependent child by a group of stupid, puffed up, superstitious, ignorant old men?'"

Well, if you live such a protected life that the only scandals you encounter occur on TV programmes, then you're in for an occasional somersault. But you and Humphrey are far from finished with this Inca outrage (remember, all along, that this supposed incident occurred a full half-millennium in the past):

> Humphrey's point – and mine – is that, regardless of whether she was a willing victim or not, there is strong reason to suppose that she would not have been willing if she had been in full possession of the facts. For example, suppose she had known that the sun is really a ball of hydrogen, hotter than a million degrees Kelvin, converting itself into helium by nuclear fusion, and that it originally formed from a disc of gas out of which the rest of the solar system, including Earth, also condensed ...

But at last we come to some semblance of a point in these ramblings, namely the suggestion that religious beliefs should not be defended on the basis that they promote cultural diver-

sity. You cite the members of the gentle Amish religious move-
ment, who live in closed communities in different parts of the
United States, many of them speaking an old German dialect,
while banning the products of the industrial revolution. Some
Amish parents came in conflict with state law three decades ago
because they took their children out of school. Eventually the
Supreme Court found in favour of the parents in the interests
of the preservation of these islands of cultural difference in
America. But the interest for Humphrey and you is whether
the children were genuinely in a position to make such decisive
judgments about their future with lasting consequences. Well,
yes, there is something of a point here – the more a community
is out of kilter with the surrounding society or culture, the
more the children are likely to lose out on future possibilities
and choices. But perhaps the Amish, who make you "feel very
queasy indeed", were not the best example to hold up to ridicule
in the scathing way that you do:

> ... you quaint little people with your bonnets and breeches,
> your horse buggies, your archaic dialect and your earth-closet
> privies, you enrich our lives. Of course you must be allowed
> to trap your children with you in your seventeenth-century
> time warp, otherwise something irretrievable would be lost
> to us: a part of the wonderful diversity of human culture.

There may come a time, sooner rather than later, when these "quaint little people" will be a living testimony to the advantages of frugality and simplicity of life, especially in a country which is devouring hugely more than its share of the planet's unrenewable resources, poisoning the environment, and squandering into the bargain the future capital and well-being of countless future generations. Is not the scandal of our time the plundering of the planet's capital of natural resources?

But before we leave the subject, let me suggest five reasons why parents should be left in peace to raise children according to the family faith, obviously within the law.

1. It is widely accepted that unless children are given the opportunity to experience religion in childhood, as they might experience music, art, and poetry, too, they are being deprived of a meaningful choice later on, since they have no sense of what they are rejecting. The reasons for this should be apparent by what follows.

2. Religion, like love and knowledge of family members, is more than just a lifestyle choice to be made in adulthood, like taking up bridge, or sky-diving: it is in many respects combined inextricably with ethnic identity, traditions, and roots that connect with every aspect of family life and culture — food, celebration of festivals, music, extended

kinship. Religion, then, is much more than a set of "beliefs", although it may at points be inseparable from them. For most believers religion is what gives life meaning, and makes life worthwhile. Most religionists would therefore consider it a form of abuse to deprive their children of its manifold benefits.

3. Religious education in childhood does not appear an obstacle to lapsing from the faith in adolescence or adulthood, even though countless examples could be forthcoming to illustrate attendant problems. The same could be said for children raised as atheists who opt to take up religion later in life. British sociologists estimate that some 1.3 million Catholics attend church in the United Kingdom today. They also estimate that if all those Irish migrants who came to this country since the First World War had continued to practise, the number of Catholic attendees would today amount to 15 million.

4. Many migrants arrive in their countries of adoption with nothing but their families and their faith, which becomes a crucial aspect of individual and group identity for people separated from their roots. On a practical level, suggestions that the atheist "intelligentsia" of developing countries are seeking to ban religious education of children would surely

be counterproductive, demonstrating that secularism is every bit as pernicious as they ever suspected it to be.

5. It is a false assumption that religious practice and beliefs across all religions are reducible to a uniquely definable norm (like an act of sexual abuse). For Catholics in some countries in Africa and South America attendance at church around Easter may be all that is possible, and sufficient to sustain religious affiliation; in Japan, Shinto practice might signify no more than visiting a shrine at New Year; for Muslims in the Middle East and North Africa it would be a pilgrimage to Mecca once in a person's lifetime; for some Christians it might be to attend a carol concert once a year. Anything so little in the scope of a norm as religious belief and practice could hardly be policed and controlled.

15

Life after Death

"Polls suggest," you write on the subject of death, "that approximately 95 per cent of the population of the United States believe they will survive their own death." I don't know which poll you are referring to, but the figure does not coincide with a wide sample of recent polls, registering closer to 74 per cent. You'll find, moreover, that a particularly reliable poll (International Social Survey) puts the figure at closer to 55 per cent. Corresponding figures in other countries are: UK, 26.5 per cent; Russia, 16.8 per cent; Italy, 34.8 per cent. The reason for the discrepancy between your figure and the International Social Survey in the United States is that people in the latter were asked whether they "definitely believed" in a life after death. The specific question is important since many religious believers express their "hope" in an afterlife, rather than "definite belief", let alone "certainty" or "certain knowledge". The only certainty mentioned in the funeral obsequies of the Catholic, Anglican, Episcopalian, and Methodist Churches is that those mourners present will themselves soon follow the same route to mortality.

For this reason I think you are perfectly justified in your comment: "I can't help wondering how many people who claim such belief [in an afterlife] really, in their heart of hearts, hold it." Interesting, that distinction between "belief" and "holding something in one's heart of hearts". A belief, and even a definite belief, is not at all the same as knowing something; being certain about something; holding something in your heart of hearts. For most religious believers, as I've tried to emphasise, belief is constantly assailed and qualified by doubt, and doubt of doubt. What lies beyond the grave is perhaps the subject of the most tenuous of all beliefs, even for committed religionists, and "hope" is generally as strong as it gets.

You, Richard, as an atheist obviously do not entertain any such hopes, yet you do seek to offer atheistic and scientific "consolations" as *substitutes* for religion's notion of an afterlife. Hence you describe a number of strategies which appear to me closer to denial of death than acceptance of it. The atheist "philosopher's" view you cite argues that when an old man dies,

"The child that he once was 'died' long ago … From this point of view, the moment when the old man finally expires is no different from the slow 'deaths' throughout his life." Tell that to a teenager dying of cancer, and his family.

And yet, you write as if you see death exclusively as an event occurring in egotistical isolation, an extinction of an individual's consciousness, rather than as a separation from loved ones: the final breaking of familial and social ties. The deaths suffered through the different stages of human life, as the "philosopher" evokes them, appear not to involve such separations. It does not seem to occur to your philosopher that death is not something that happens just to *you*; it happens also to those close to you – who remain behind.

These separations in death occur whether one hopes for the resurrection of the body or not. Jesus on the cross in his dying words acknowledged acceptance of death as an intimate human separation, which is why he recommends his mother and the beloved disciple to each other; his final words expressed the agony of separation even from the Father: "My God, my God, why hast thou forsaken me!" The death of Jesus is not about the loss of personal ego, but about the finality of relationships severed in death.

You raise the question, however: what consolation for a dying person can science afford? You quote yourself (who else?) from your book *The Devil's Chaplain*:

There is more than just grandeur in this view of life, bleak and cold though it can seem from under the security blanket of ignorance. There is deep refreshment to be had from standing up and facing straight into the strong keen wind of understanding: Yeats's 'Winds that blow through the starry ways'.

This final thought, it appears, is an act of egoistical defiance, as the dying person gazes gimlet-eyed into the vast, awesome, meaningless galaxies. Austerely impressive. Nonetheless, I have to question the appropriateness of your quotation from Yeats's poem, which is entitled "To My Heart, Bidding It Have No Fear" (1899), written when the poet was aged thirty-four, and deeply involved in ancient magic and theosophy. The entire poem is as follows:

Be you still, be you still, trembling heart;
Remember the wisdom out of the old days:
Him who trembles before the flame and the flood,
And the winds that blow through the starry ways,
Let the starry winds and the flame and the flood
Cover over and hide, for he has no part
With the proud, majestical multitude.

There is little doubt that the wisdom out of the "old days"

refers to Yeats's interest in esoteric knowledge, of which his
father and many friends thoroughly disapproved. The "Him"
invoked in the poem is the object of the verb "Let". Thus, he
who goes in fear of the natural world – fire, flood, and hurricane
– should be swallowed up by them, for he is incapable of enjoy-
ing the "proud, majestical multitude", which those acquainted
with Yeats will immediately recognise as the vast world of phan-
toms, ghosts, and spirits with which he was striving to connect
during this period.

Far be it from me to question what you should take from
a poem, but it seems strange that you should enlist the great
modern poet of mysticism as your guide into the darkness:
hardly an exponent of a positivist vision of the universe. And
yet, for all his youthful pursuit of the occult, Yeats, when it
came to facing his own death, was not one to seek consolations
in philosophy, mysticism, or human reasoning, let alone the
grandeur of the universe as perceived by science. In the last
year of his life, forty years after the poem you quote, he wrote
a poem entitled "The Man and the Echo":

> O Rocky Voice,
> Shall we in that great night rejoice?
> What do we know but that we face
> One another in this place?
> But hush, for I have lost the theme,

It's joy or night seem but a dream;
Up there some hawk or owl has struck,
Dropping out of sky or rock,
A stricken rabbit is crying out,
And its cry distracts my thought.

There is no leading thought, certainly no final consolation, but a combination of "themes" playing off each other. The poet, speaking on behalf of humankind, consults the Oracle on what lies "beyond". The question can be interpreted in different ways. "Should we rejoice on contemplating the great night of the universe?" "Will we rejoice in accepting the great night of annihilation that death brings?" "Will we find rejoicing in the life beyond death?" What comes back is the voice of mankind's own questioning echo. There are no answers, no consolations; the only certainty is that of human relationships as "we face one another in this place". But all ultimate questions are drowned out by the scream of a dying animal. Humankind can think, dream, question, speculate, but the only absolute certainty is that of human relationships attended by the insoluble problem of violent and suffering nature.

Religious believers are no less spared such meditations than atheistic scientists.

16

Religious People Less Clever Than Atheists?

Under the guise of discussing the prevalence, or otherwise, of religious belief among scientists, you suggest that religious believers are less clever than atheistic scientists. I suppose that could be true; but I am fascinated by the stages of your logic.

You start by quoting Bertrand Russell again: "... intellectually eminent men disbelieve in Christian religion," you quote him as saying, "but they conceal the fact in public, because they are afraid of losing their incomes."

Quite apart from the provincialism of this (what of eminent Jewish, Muslim, Hindu, and Sikh men), I wondered about bringing in Russell from the outset, as if he were a self-evident expert on the matter. Russell was surely an important figure in philosophy or mathematics, but didn't he also say some pernicious things outside his area of expertise, especially on the subject of intelligence? For example: "Women are on the average stupider than men." Just because Bertrand Russell says something doesn't mean to say that it's true.

Russell's view is plain: that public profession of faith is determined not by true conviction but by how it affects a person's career and financial prospects. Which is odd: for when you come to parade the absence of religious belief among eminent scientists you appear to have abandoned this claim for self-interested discretion. You make a different point: that the evident scarcity of self-proclaimed religionists among scientists shows that scientists are just too clever to be believers. And yet, Russell's generalisation could be applied also to the eminent scientists, could it not? Let's do it in the form of a simple syllogism:

1. The willingness of eminent intellectuals to be truthful about their religious convictions (or the lack of them) is dictated by how it might affect their career prospects.

2. Eminent scientists (who might also be characterised as eminent intellectuals) tend to profess atheism rather than religious belief.

3. Therefore scientists are professing their atheism merely in order to protect their career prospects.

But, of course, you do not intend your readers to draw this inference. Mind you, I think there might be a straw of unpleasant truth in Russell's view. Where atheism and science predominate in colleges and university departments nowadays, prejudice is often in evidence. You earlier described to your readers an occasion when the head of your Oxford college humiliated (with your apparent approval) a young research fellowship candidate because his topic happened to be a study of religion (although you don't tell us what the study was about).

Pretty well every page of your book exhibits this kind of prejudice against religious believers. I wondered, I must say, about your attempt to make public mockery of three distinguished British scientists – the late Professor Arthur Peacocke, Professor Russell Stannard, and Professor John Polkinghorne. Their crime? They see no conflict between being a scientist and professing religious faith. These three men crop up, you tell us, like "senior partners in a firm of Dickensian lawyers: Peacocke, Stannard and Polkinghorne". Not a bad joke, except that far more scientists than this trio are both scientists and religious believers, as you acknowledge. We might as well say that you and your atheist friends, Peter Atkins and Daniel Dennett, crop up with all the familiarity of a provincial firm of insurance brokers: "Dawkins, Atkins, and Dennett".

You move on now to argument by anecdote. You tell your readers that you had a conversation in the garden of Clare College, Cambridge, with James Watson, the "founding genius of the Human Genome Project". You asked him whether he knew many religious scientists today. An excellent person to ask, he being both a genius and counting many scientists among his acquaintance. Here was his answer: "'Virtually none. Occasionally I meet them, and I'm a bit embarrassed [laughs] because, you know, I can't believe anyone accepts truth by revelation.'"

You must admit that such a view might as well have been advanced late into the evening over several pints by any of the denizens of the Mitre pub in Bridge Street, Cambridge.

Next you produce your clincher. Apparently Watson's co-founder of the molecular genetics revolution, the late Francis Crick, resigned his fellowship at Churchill College, Cambridge, "because of the college's decision to build a chapel (at the behest of a benefactor)". I suppose that took a lot of courage. Yet I doubt that it did much harm to Crick's career and financial prospects; and one has to ask whether you really believe that Crick and Watson's discovery of the molecular structure of DNA has a bearing on their anecdotal pronouncements on religion, society, morality, or any other subject outside molecular biology. These two, famous for their scientistic atheism, have unburdened themselves of two remarkable opinions. Watson recently advocated that human embryos genetically testing positive for bi-polar depression should be aborted. And Crick informed the world: "You, your joys and your sorrows, your memories and your ambitions, your sense of personal identity and free will, are in fact no more than the behaviour of a vast assembly of nerve cells and their associated molecules." Stout fellows.

Then you claim that religious believers are in short supply among Britain's top scientists – the Fellows of the Royal Society – and among the members of the Mensa society, the British-founded club for people with high IQ scores. But are not scientists, and self-selecting groups such as Mensa members, apt to display particular kinds of intelligence quite distinct from, say, philosophers, artists, musicians, writers, bankers, actuaries, medical practitioners, novelists, poets, concert pianists, historians, theologians, and anthropologists? I don't want to dismiss your argument out of hand, but why should anybody take scientists, or the Mensa society, as representing the cream of intellect and imagination, any more than bond-traders, chess-players, pawnbrokers, or cardinals in the Vatican? Each of these callings in life quite obviously represents a specific range of aptitudes. Hence the argument is reduced instantly by applying it in a parallel category: the Jesuits, for example. Jesuits are widely deemed smart and well-educated, quite independently of the Catholic Church. But very few Jesuits, if any, turn out to be scientists; fewer still are atheists, and there are no Jesuit women. Should we therefore take it that atheists, scientists, and women are unlikely to be intellectually eminent?

It's that undistributed middle. Which pops up again when you come to Nobel Prize-winners, citing a study that claims: "'among Nobel Prize laureates in the sciences, as well as those in literature, there was a remarkable degree of irreligiosity, as compared to the populations they came from'".

So what's this religiosity? Does it cover being a Sabbath-observing Jew or Christian? Or an occasional mosque-goer? Does it cover marriage in the local church? Does it apply to belief or mere practice? Exhibiting religiosity, according to most dictionaries, signifies not normal religious practice or belief but morbid or sentimental religious behaviour, or excess of religiousness. One should not be surprised that individuals who spend their lives in laboratories pursuing highly focused research programmes in the natural sciences would have little time, appetite, or scope for religiosity.

And let's look more widely at the inferences we could draw. By the year 1920 more than 50 per cent of all Nobel Prize-winners in the natural sciences were Germans. Does this mean that the Germans through this period were cleverer than all other nationalities? By the same token, women have consist-ently been overlooked by the Nobel panel: again, does this mean that women are less capable of genius in science? Well, we happen to know all too many scandalous cases of women being deprived of their just deserts by the Nobel panel. They include the German-Jewish physicist Lisa Meitner, who should have shared the prize with Otto Hahn for the discovery of fission, and Rosalind Franklin, who should have shared the Watson–Crick prize for the discovery of the structure of DNA.

17

Does Our Moral Sense Have a Darwinian Origin?

It is high time we took a look at your explanations for the origins of apparent goodness in the form of selflessness: why it is that individuals appear capable of being "altruistic, generous or 'moral' towards each other"? Your aim, of course, is to demolish the idea that belief in God and religion might have anything to do with being good.

Your explanation for apparent altruism (apparent, since you believe altruism to be selfishness masquerading as altruism) is based on Darwin's theory of evolution, and not surprisingly you invoke your famous characterisation of our genes as "selfish". Since human beings are mere vehicles for their gene pools –

which are predetermined to act in the interests of their own survival – in what sense, you ask, can the human "organism" act altruistically, generously, morally, unselfishly? If a man dives into a river to save his daughter from being drowned, thereby risking his own life, he may well believe that this is proof of altruistic love for his daughter; in your view, however, he is merely acting in the interests of the future survival of his genes.

But what of wider acts of apparent unselfishness, within the extended family, friends, colleagues, clients, and charitable acts towards people one has never met: gifts for the starving in Africa, for example? According to you there are four reasons – each underpinned, and determined, by Darwin's theory.

First, there is the kindness displayed between members of the same family – explained by wider preservation of kinship genes. Second, there is hope of reciprocation: Margaret gives Sophie a present in the office in the hope that she'll get one back. Third, generosity can build a person's reputation and hence expectation of special treatment. Finally, reputation for generosity can result in greater power within the group: one might call it self-paid advertisements for oneself. So is there no escape from this natural law of selfishness? Here you play your evolutionary "by-product" card once more: only this time you call it "a misfiring".

"In a bird's brain," you tell your readers, "the rule 'Look after small squawking things in your nest, and drop food into their red gapes' typically has the effect of preserving the genes that built the rule, because the squawking, gaping objects in an adult bird's nest are normally its own offspring." There is "a misfiring" if an alien baby bird, such as a cuckoo, gets into the nest and mother bird finds herself working in the interests of the trespasser.

In other words the strong urge to self-sacrifice in the interests of gene preservation persists even when the normal objects of attention, offspring, are absent. "We can no more help ourselves feeling pity when we see a weeping unfortunate ... than we can help ourselves feeling lust for a member of the opposite sex (who may be infertile or otherwise unable to reproduce)." The underpinning explanation is identical with your explanation for religious behaviour, which you claim to be a "by-product" of a genetic disposition for a child to believe cautionary tales even when they have no basis of truth in the real world.

Then you claim that there is no statistical difference between an atheist and a religious believer when both are faced with moral dilemmas. The dilemmas you raise are as follows.

1. Some 90 per cent of people said that it was permissible to perform an act that indirectly killed one person in order to save the lives of five people (this is the well-known double-effect — my *intention* was not to kill one person; it was an unfortunate effect of the action of saving five lives, rather than intentionally killing that one person).

2. Some 97 per cent of people said that they would save a child drowning in a pond even though it meant ruining their trousers.

3. Some 97 per cent of people also agree that it would be morally wrong to kill one individual in order to supply organ parts for five other patients.

Yet these stock moral dilemmas hardly exhaust the infinite range of goodness (and evil) performed by human beings, nor do they tell us much, if anything, about the quality and range of altruism (or of evil). For religious believers, moreover, it is not their *belief* in God, but *God*, that makes them good: God's presence, whose goodness tames the egoism, vanity, and violence of the human heart. Unlike Dostoyevsky's vision, the landscape of your ethical imagination bears no hint of the true tragedy and darkness of the world.

18

The Darwinian Imperative

I want to come back to your reading of Darwin and religion. "Knowing that we are products of Darwinian evolution," you write, "we should ask what pressure or pressures exerted by natural selection favoured the impulse to religion." Well, there's a lot to be said for Charles Darwin's theory of natural selection as an explanation for the origin of species. But only a double-dyed fundamentalist Darwinian would deny that an evolutionary perspective furnishes no more than a slender contribution to what drives human behaviour, especially in the cultural sphere of the imaginative, the poetic, the artistic.

You yourself, let's not forget, have argued in *The Selfish Gene* that human beings, armed with imagination and the ability to envisage future options, can rebel against the "tyranny of the replicators". Hence you will surely accept that anything so complex, social, diverse, and protean as religious behaviour, in all its vast array of manifestations, is hardly reducible to a single description explicable by genetic determinism within natural selection.

So the claim that "universal features of a species *demand* a Darwinian explanation" pushes the envelope more in terms of propaganda than of science. You claim that religious behaviour is a "writ-large human equivalent" of animal behaviour such as bower-building or beaver dam construction. And you have famously claimed that the dam may be regarded as part of the beaver's phenotype – thus absorbing an entire complex, multi-dimensional universe of the organism in its natural setting into a one-dimensional single strand of DNA. Yet even if there were merit in this view of genes and function, there is a crucial difference between religious behaviour and bower-building. I suspect that you have a clear notion of what counts as bower-building, or dam-building by beavers, or the making of ant-hills; but there is little agreement among the experts as to what does and does not count as "religion". And this is quite apart from the fact that anything so complex, social, and demanding of human imagination, relationships, and choices as religion defies reducibility to a single principle.

Conscious of this, perhaps, you fall back on the shaky parallel, suggested by your friend Daniel Dennett, between the peacock's tail and wasteful expenditure of energy on religious manifestations. You cite the case of the medieval cathedral, which, you claim, "was never used as a dwelling, or for any recognizably useful purpose". But by what criterion of usefulness? Cathedrals have been "employed" since their inception as the "mother churches" of a diocese, a place that draws in the clergy and faithful under their bishop – hence a specific kind of assembly point, as well as a focus for special religious celebrations, including weddings, funerals, musical performances, and coronations. They have been used as places of burial, of sanctuary, and as shrines of national identity and unity. Cathedrals stand as great works of architectural art in their own right. We can take it, in any case, that the peacock is in no sense responsible for its plumage, whereas the architects, builders, and patrons of the great medieval projects were all too conscious of their expenditure of treasure, time, and energy, its purposes and its manifold advantages – aesthetic, cultural, and mythical. To deny the "usefulness" of a cathedral, any more than you would deny the usefulness of a theatre, a bar, a dance hall, a cinema, fashion clothes, or jewellery, is like Goneril's splenetic reproach of King Lear for his "useless" retinue; to which he replies:

> *O, reason not the need! Our basest beggars*
> *Are in the poorest thing superfluous.*
> *Allow not nature more than nature needs,*
> *Man's life's as cheap as beast's. Thou art a lady:*
> *If only to go warm were gorgeous,*
> *Why, nature needs not what thou gorgeous wear'st,*
> *Which scarcely keeps thee warm …*

To ram home your rationale, however, you now proceed to a philosophy of explanations. The ultimate explanation for "the explosion in the cylinder of an internal combustion engine," you write, concerns "the purpose for which the explosion was designed". In the same way your ultimate explanation for religious behaviour is to be found in evolution, as I outlined at the start of my letter – as a by-product of the cautionary tale, belief in which carries a survival advantage when there is an element of truth in the fiction, but which can also result in giving credence to dangerous untruths.

Without rehearsing your Darwinian argument, I want to explore with you this notion of "ultimate explanation", which you insist is concerned with the *purposes* of *design*. For a strict Darwinist this is a curious statement. The point of the "blind watchmaker" principle, whereby you earned your reputation as a leading expositor of Darwin's theory of evolution, is that there is no "teleology" in nature – in other words, no grand designer, no purpose; it is *blind*. You, yourself, later define teleology as "the assignment of purpose to everything". And you have already stated, "uncertainty as to details doesn't – nor should it – stop Darwinians from presuming, with great confidence, that anting [for example] must be 'for' something." I've noticed that you sometimes put these scare quotes around your more heretical teleological statements; but I'm sorry, scare quotes do not let you off the hook of teleological incorrectness.

Your addiction to teleological explanations of natural functions, in total antithesis to what you affect to teach about evolution, is patently unscientific, as are your teleological "remote" evolutionary explanations for cultural and social behaviour. I'm aware that you believe your anthropomorphisms to be useful teaching tools, but I see that you employ them even in academic studies: terms such as "purpose", "need", "easy", "improvement", "designed", "welfare", "good", "advantage" recur repeatedly in your professional scientific writing. Yet you know better than anybody that assigning purpose to objects, systems, and organisms, outside human societies, is purely subjective, since purpose does not exist outside the mind. The explosion in the cylinder of the combustion engine is known only to its designer and not to the system. The exquisite symmetry, complexity, precision, of living things – from a molecule to a human brain – may seem to proclaim a designer, and yet there is clearly no designer in the sense that there is for a human artefact, as you teach. It may seem that the nest-building of birds, or the dam-building of beavers, ant-hills, and thrushes' nests, indicates a sense of highly complex subjective intention. But the whole point of nature's "imagination", conscious human ingenuity apart, is that the mechanism of evolution, purged of teleology, provides an alternative, powerful explanation for the diversity and exquisite complexity of the living world. So how come that you, more than most expositors of biology, consistently assign intentions, subjectivism, strategies, designer-motives to nature right down to the molecule? As David Hanke, one of your Cambridge colleagues, has put it: "One major reason is the manner in which Natural Selection slipped seamlessly into the place of the Creator: the Natural Selector as the acceptable new face of the Great Designer. Darwin drew on examples of domestication as the major source of evidence for his theory. The Human Selector, full of purpose, was the model of the Natural Selector – just substitute the Natural World for the Pigeon Fancier." Natural Selection has become the new divinity for the Dawkinesque evolutionists.

While the God Natural Selector is perhaps an unconscious tendency (at least, one hopes this to be so), your Darwinian enthusiasm as applied to human behaviour – sexual behaviour, intelligence, imagination, religious belief – has become a story about reductive explanation. In your vision of the origin, survival, and death of species you see the organism – for example, the elephant, the water beetle, or a human being — as a "lumbering robot", a vehicle for the replication of its genes, and in the case of human beings, its "memes". Hence, it is not surprising, thirty years on from the publication of *The Selfish Gene,* that molecular geneticists increasingly see individual human beings as assemblies of determined gene, and meme, functions.

19

Religion as a Bacillus

One of your constant and most controversial arguments for explaining the spread and tenacity of religious beliefs is based on parallels between natural selection and the growth of culture. You began this comparison in *The Selfish Gene* by drawing an analogy between genes and the transmission of ideas and cultural traits in general; but, when it suits, you adopt the metaphor of memes as an infection following the lead of your associate Dr Nicholas Humphrey, who preferred the notion of the transmission of ideas as viruses. In *The God Delusion* you write about a particular "memetic" craze for making origamis, paper Chinese junks, which you introduced to a school, where it spread like "a measles epidemic". Daniel Dennett also employs the genes and virus models (as if the two entities were equivalent). But whether gene or a virus, commentators have found problems with understanding cultural entities in this way.

If an idea, such as the idea of God or a god, can be thought of as parallel to a gene it would mean that beliefs come in discrete packages. But this hardly makes sense since ideas, and especially religion, are generally untidy with multiple relationships and differences in complexity, emotions, depth of intellectual rigour, associations, and so forth. The word "god" expresses a diversity of meanings, depending on cultural, philosophical, ethnic, and historical background. Belief itself, moreover, comes in a variety of shades of assent – from absolute conviction and commitment, to vague speculation bordering on scepticism. The anthropologist Adam Kuper puts it like this: "Unlike genes, cultural traits are not particulate. An idea about God cannot be separated from other ideas with which it is indissolubly linked in a particular religion."

A crucial quality of your meme notion is that it replicates, like a gene or an antigen. In other words memes make copies of themselves which spread and thrive in environments advantageous to reproduction. Yet while it is undeniable that ideas spread among people, exceptionally rapidly at times, it is by no means clear that they do this in a manner similar to biological replication. When a person thinks about a god, or God, every conception of that idea, special to that person, comes as a new act of imagination, or memory, rather than an item of received and mutant information. The same is true of the passing of ideas between members of a group or population.

Henry Plotkin, professor of psychobiology at University College London, puts it nicely: "The gene is structurally inert ... [but] the meme as a memory is dynamic and transient and no one has any idea how neural network states are reconstituted to form memories, whether of actions, words, faces or anything else ... The inert-versus-dynamic and copy-versus-reconstitute differences appear to be serious dis-analogies, and these are not the only ones."

A religious believer's idea of God, throughout a lifetime, from childhood to old age, is bound to be one of expanding, and sometimes contracting, associations, including original ideas, concepts, and metaphors, some of which have been initiated by the believer rather than received. Belief might include even the rejection of a repertoire of unacceptable notions about God. So a person's idea of God does not have a single lineage, as is the case with genes, or viruses, but develops imaginatively, creatively, and dynamically with the ebb and flow of relationships, reading, chance encounters, age, and life experience.

Another objection raises the possibility of alternative models. The Cambridge philosopher of Darwinism Tim Lewens puts it succinctly:

It is unclear how much the meme insight brings that could not be had just as well by using models from psychology or economics. This is not to say that no cultural evolutionary theory has value, but such theories need to examine how ideas are reproduced, how they mutate, how the structure of a population of ideas affects the prospects of that population and so forth. These are the kinds of questions that needed to be answered before Darwin's theory of natural selection could be applied in a detailed manner to organic evolution, and the same questions need to be asked in the cultural realm.

But another consideration arises. Obviously there can be benign bacteria and harmful ones. You have maintained for some years, however, that religious beliefs are in the main not simply deleterious for those individuals who hold them, but are infectiously dangerous for society and human flourishing as a whole. You have written of those "afflicted with the mental virus of faith, and its accompanying gang of secondary infections", while insisting that scientific ideas do not share such malignancy, for "they do not favour pointless self-serving behaviour". Here are some of the descriptions you apply to religious believers:

... malevolent ... propagandist ... mischief-stirring ... obscurantist ... vicious, sado-masochistic and repellent ...

barking mad ... viciously unpleasant ... mendacious ... obnoxious ... vindictive ... dodgy ... deluded ... mawk- ishly nauseating ... perniciously delusional ... ditzy ... unreal ... slavish ... gullible ... fatuous ...indoctrinated ... brainwashed ... fanatical ... absolutist ... sanctimoni- ously hypocritical ... cockeyed ...

To apply, in addition, the model of a harmful infectious disease to religious belief may seem harmless enough as a mental exer- cise in a university seminar room; but the implications of such a model require careful examination, since the analogy of infection suggests certain unspoken remedies, antidotes, and solutions.

I am not suggesting that you would have anything but con- tempt and loathing for the "bio-political" ideas that arose in Nazi Germany in the 1920s and 1930s; but I want to impress on you the far-reaching potential consequences of likening believers, or any group of people in society, to disease-carriers.

We expect that replicators will go around together from brain to brain in mutually compatible gangs. These gangs will come to constitute a package, which may be sufficiently stable to deserve a collective name such as Roman Catholi- cism or Voodoo. It doesn't much matter whether we analo- gise the whole package to a single virus, or each one of the component parts to a single part.

The implication of depersonalisation and identification of groups of individuals with a single dangerous disease is clear. There have been occasions in the past when you were specific about the harm that resides in the faith virus (for example, the invocation of the fatwa against Salman Rushdie), but in *The God Delusion* you make it clear that faith, any kind of faith, of any degree whatsoever, however mild, is a viral infection of equivalent danger:

> The take-home message is that we should blame religion itself, not religious *extremism* – as though that were some kind of terrible perversion of real, decent religion ... This is one reason why I do everything in my power to warn people against faith itself, not just against so-called "extremist" faith. The teachings of "moderate" religion, though not extremist in themselves, are an open invitation to extremism.

The shocking aspect of this, however, is the implication as to how this disease, which reduces individuals and groups of individuals to a "single virus", might be eradicated.

If religious memes can behave like harmful viruses, then the obvious solution is quarantining with a view to the protection of society and the ultimate control and elimination of the disease. Your friend and meme-theory associate Daniel Dennett has actually employed not only the quarantining image, but an association even more harsh – the cage. "My own spirit sinks when I see a lion pacing neurotically back and forth in a small zoo cage," he has written. "I know, I know, the lion is beautiful but dangerous; if you let the lion roam free, it would kill me. Safety demands that religions be put in cages, too – when absolutely necessary." Dennett goes on to cite specifically those religions that tend to extremism in their practices; but you hold with no such distinction between benign and malefic religion. And even if Dennett appears on the face of it more modest in his proposal about the categories of those to be caged, there remains the question as to who decides which beliefs are dangerous and which are not. Dennett proclaims: "There are no forces on this planet more dangerous to us all than the fanaticisms of fundamentalism, of all the species: Protestantism, Catholicism, Judaism, Islam, Hinduism, and Buddhism, as well as countless smaller infections." So who is to decide what constitutes fundamentalism? You have already decided: it is any form of faith, however mild.

My main quarrel with your meme theory, then, is that you have adapted it to represent religious believers as "vectors", carriers, of an infection or parasite that mortally threatens the healthy body of a society or culture: you single out children, moreover, as being especially in danger, reserving, for example, your particular loathing for teaching nuns. You draw analogies between faith and medical models. "In the history of the spread of faith," you write, "you will find little else but epidemiology and causal epidemiology at that." You refer to faith as a "handicap", and point to its deleterious "symptoms". You refer to believers as "faith sufferers", and you refer to you and your associates as "we doctors". The precedents of such analogies, which carry the implication of certain groups being labelled as aliens, have hardly been innocuous in recent history. Nazi ideology subscribed from the very outset to the idea of the German people as a type of anatomy subject to alien people operating as diseases. It harped on the introduction of undesirable extraneous influences on the healthy Nordic body, the *Volkskörper*, behaving like pathogens and bacilli: analogies of quarantines, cures, surgery, and purgings naturally followed. As early as 1925 Hitler lamented the fact that the state did not have the means to "master the disease" which was penetrating the "bloodstream of our people unhindered". Such ideas, bogus as they were pernicious, culled from medical analogies inevitably referred to the new leadership as "healers". By the mid-1930s the ideological bio-political content of Nazism merged with Nazi medical science. The Nazi plenipotentiary Dr Gerhard Wagner wrote of the *völkisch* body being in need of "cleansing", while the language of "immunity" and "radical therapy" became routine. Your recourse to the analogies of medicine is, of course, entirely well-meaning; but have you and your colleagues considered the far-reaching consequences of less well-meaning use of metaphors?

Beyond Dennett's "cage" and Humphrey's insistence that religious education undermines the human rights of children, there is no clear indication among you and your anti-religious associates as to how you would eliminate religion in order to create a better society. You leave your readers in little doubt, however, that should you ever acquire political influence or actual power, your policies would inevitably follow from your vision of faith as a disease.

20

Does God Exist?

There is clearly a difference between a religious apprehension of God involving beliefs, sacred books, prayers, and
ceremonies, and those purely rational enquiries made by philosophers that lead to a wager on the probability, or perhaps
improbability, of the existence of a Creator. You, like others
over the past three hundred years, have taken the latter path and
found God improbable. As you put it: "there almost certainly is
no God." Yet across a span of 3,000 years from Plato and Aristotle in ancient Greece to Alfred North Whitehead and Ludwig
Wittgenstein in the twentieth century, there have been philosophers whose investigations, while not proving God's existence

definitively, have failed to find the world to be godless. What kind of defence might a philosopher, unaided by faith, religious experience, and revelation, make of a Creator that renders the deep and ultimate mystery of the world intelligible? An angel, with direct knowledge of God, obviously sees things differently. Only a mortal can explain to another mortal how God might be apprehended philosophically, if only on the remote horizon of human consciousness.

There was a brilliant Dominican friar, the late Father Herbert McCabe, who made it his life's work – with the aid of the thinking of Thomas Aquinas – to explain what it means to assert the existence of God. You will forgive me if I adopt his favoured populist mode of argument – which, I hope, will contain some surprises. Father McCabe's starting point is that proving the existence of God does not expect a conclusion. It is an ongoing, never-ending process, rather like proving the valid-ity of science – not any particular facts in science, but science as an authentic activity of provisional discoveries and theories: an endless questioning venture into the unknown.

Philosophical proofs for the existence of God similarly involve endless questioning. If it is all right for science to ask "How come?" about particular things or events in the world, why should it be wrong to ask "How come?" about the exist-ence of the entire world? As Father McCabe puts it: "Can we be puzzled by the existence of the world instead of nothing?"

Obviously a mortal can be, and often is, puzzled about that question: why is there something rather than nothing? For Father McCabe, this is what it means to be puzzled about the existence of God.

How does this work?

Suppose I ask: "How come your Labrador dog, Spot?" I could be asking whether Spot was sired by a known champion dog and bitch with papers, or whether he was an accident of the mongrel across the street. The question is not problematic, nor, given sufficient enquiry, is the answer. But what if I ask: "How come that Spot is a dog?" I have moved the "why" or "how come" question onto a different level: a question about the origin of species, which has been extensively answered by Charles Darwin, Gregor Mendel, and others through the past century. The question is still about Spot, your individual dog, but now it is about Spot's membership of a wider community, a biological group to which dogs belong. Well, the "how come" questions, and answers, don't stop here. Going to further levels, the questions would eventually involve biochemistry, and ultimately physics and the laws of the universe following the Big Bang. I could put all this in another way: "How come Spot is this dog rather than another; he's the champion dog and bitch's son rather than the mongrel over the road? At the next level: How come he's a dog rather than a cat? And at the next level: How come he's a living creature rather than an inanimate piece of material?" And so on.

All these questions relate still to Spot, but each new level raises a question relating to what it is for Spot to come to be by noting what he is not, but might have been. Every question, moreover, is "why as opposed to why not", and every question relates to an existing reality or state of affairs by virtue of which Spot is as opposed to what he is not.

And there is an ultimate, radical question, which has not yet been reached: and that is, simply, why does such a being as Spot exist instead of *nothing*? This question puts Spot not just in relation to parents, species, animate or inanimate matter, but *everything*, the entire universe or world. Why is there something rather than nothing?

This is the God-question.

Some philosophers and scientists have sought to dismiss (that is, not ask) this ultimate "How come?" question by riposting, as did Bertrand Russell, that the universe is there because it is just there, which seems as arbitrary as to say that dogs are there just because they are there. Now, it is true that Charles Darwin's great theory has given us an answer to the question "Why Spot?" of a kind that is now familiar, so that it would be entirely arbitrary to answer it by saying, "He's just there." But isn't Russell's insouciant dismissal also arbitrary in its way? The question is altogether *un*familiar and not of the same kind – how come there is a world rather than nothing at all? – and to raise it is to embark on an unending quest. As the philosopher Ludwig Wittgenstein said: "Not *how* the world is, but *that* it is, is the mystical."

It is difficult to think of the idea of "everything", since all the things that we know have a notional boundary around them: Spot is a dog and not a cat, for example. But a way of thinking about everything is to consider it as bounded by *nothing*: in other words, not bounded by anything. But it is also difficult to think of *nothing*, in an absolute sense. We tend to use the word relatively: as in, there's nothing in the cupboard, or nothing between Folkestone and Calais; but we don't *really* mean nothing. As Father McCabe puts it: "this means we are asking our ultimate radical question with tools that will not do the job properly, with words whose meaning has to be stretched beyond what we can comprehend." Or, as Wittgenstein puts it, we are encountering *the* mystery.

The question how come anything as opposed to nothing is one that stretches human beings to their limits: they reach out but never attain the answer. Some of the answers are self-evidently unsatisfactory. For example, if God is the answer to the question "How come everything?" then he is not included in that everything. God cannot be an object competing for your attention among other objects in the universe. God and the universe do not add up to two. Nor does God make the universe out of anything; for whatever God's creation may be it is not a process of making. Nor does God *interfere* in the universe, since

He would have to be an alternative to, or alongside, what He was interfering with. Being the cause of everything, however, there is nothing that He is outside of. Hence there is no feature of the universe which indicates that it is God-made. What God accounts for is that the universe is there instead of nothing.

Of course this is a point at which a philosopher might ask: "How come God in the first place?" But by definition He must contain within himself the reason for His own existence: it is not possible for Him to be nothing. Since He is not part of the universe, though, God must therefore be in everything that happens and everything that exists in the universe. If Spot's parents made him exist instead of nothing it was because God was acting in their action, just as a pen writes because the writer is acting. "Every action in the world is an action of God," writes Father McCabe, following Thomas Aquinas, "not because it is not an action of a creature but because it is by God's action that the creature is *itself* and has its *own* activity."

The ultimate fallacy of your position, and Russell's, is that you confuse two quite different areas of discourse, the scientific and the religious. You ask to see evidence, give me the evidence and I will believe, you say, no matter how surprised you would be. But the question 'Why is there anything rather than nothing?' is not a final bid for evidence but a quest for meaning or sense that has begun in a moment of wonder that there is anything at all. You ridicule the quest because you do not seem to understand it. If you understood it, you would not ridicule it even if you felt unable to go there yourself. That you do not understand it is shown by the fact that you actually think that this "argument for God" is an argument for the ludicrous anthropomorphic deity that rightly appals you. If denying this claim, as you do, is what makes a person an atheist, then most Christian theologians, including Thomas Aquinas, Father McCabe, and yours truly, can also be characterised as atheists.

A real atheist, like yourself, is one who does not accept that the question 'Why is there anything rather than nothing?' is a genuine question. You are content to ask the question within the world, but you can't see that the existence of the world raises a profound question: again, as Martin Rees, following Wittgenstein, has put it: "The preeminent mystery is why anything exists at all. What breathes life into the equations of physics, and actualized them in a real cosmos? Such questions lie beyond science, however: they are the province of philosophers and theologians."

Philosophers through the ages have invoked the possibility of God as the answer to the existence, as opposed to the non-existence, of the universe: and *creation* is the name given to the notion of its coming into being. By the same analogy creation is also the word given to the exercise whereby a poem, a piece of music, a painting, a sculpture, is brought into existence by the artist. As Father McCabe writes: "I can show, by pointing to the existence of bricks and cement and so on and the availability of a workforce, that there could be more houses made. I cannot show that there will ever be another poem."

You insist throughout your book that the existence, or non-existence, of God is a scientific question. But I hope that it is evident that I am using the word "creation" in a different sense from the way it is normally used by scientists who are seeking to discover the origin of the universe (studies of the Big Bang and so on). The enquiries of cosmologists, fascinating as they are, are irrelevant to the question of creation in the sense of why there is something rather than nothing. At the same time, being convinced that there is a Creator God leaves unanswered the scientific questions about what kind of universe it is and the story of its beginnings and development within time. The knowledge that the universe is dependent on God does not tell us anything about science since everything we know about God is derived from what we know of the universe. If we think that we can come back from God with additional information about the world it is only because we have introduced, smuggled, something extra into our notion of God – when we make God in our own image and likeness. We can speak of God's existence, and we can say what He is not. But if we speak of God as having thoughts, or making decisions, or having a strong right arm, or an all-seeing eye, it can only be by way of metaphor.

Is it possible for human beings to have a relationship with

such a God? I have been speaking of the God of the philosophers, a process of asking questions that leads to a conviction
about the possible existence or non-existence of a Creator. To
speak of involvement with God is not the business of philosophy any more than it is the business of science: it is a matter
for religion.

2 1

Being Religious

There is a story about the origins of modern atheism that you do not tell. As far back as the seventeenth century, long before the arguments proposed in *The God Delusion*, the philosopher Francis Bacon protested against the corruption of natural philosophy by theology, and in particular the practice of founding science on the first chapter of Genesis. "From this unwholesome mixture of things human and divine," he wrote, "there arises not only a fantastic philosophy but also a heretical religion." In other words it was not necessary for the advent of Charles Darwin to grasp that the Genesis story of creation was not a literal story about the creation of the world. But during the period known as the Enlightenment – through the seventeenth and eighteenth centuries in Europe – a tendency arose precisely from the opposite direction in order to answer the sort of objections raised by Bacon and his contemporaries. Two natural philosophers, Denis Diderot and Paul Henri d'Holbach, invoked atheism in reaction to theology's continued sway over physics, mathematics, and medicine. These philosophers, and they were not the only ones, were convinced that the autonomy of the sciences must be achieved by denying the existence of God. Thrown on the defensive, theology began to alienate its own nature by generating defensive forms of philosophy as apologetics. Instead of philosophy founding itself on religion, religion became increasingly founded on philosophy, and the result was a resort to theism (assent to an impersonal prime-mover divorced from religious belief and practice), or its denial – atheism. It is arguable therefore that modern atheism found its origins not so much in the demolition of God by science, as by the self-imposed alienation of defensive religion. Christian theology now tended to seek its vindication not within religious experience, event, personal witness, its own history, but in philosophy. Theological reflection brought religion under the auspices of philosophy in order to bolster religion's claims. But religion cannot justify itself, nor survive, such a reduction. In justifying its claims religion became an encouragement to atheism. The very forces mustered against atheism tended to generate religion's own vulnerability, just as the northern tribes enlisted to defend Rome and its empire eventually occupied the city and swept the empire away.

That great troubled figure Blaise Pascal, the seventeenth-century mathematician and philosopher, made this point prophetically in relation to Christianity: "All of those who seek God apart from Christ, and who go no further than nature, either find no light to satisfy them or come to devise a means of knowing and serving God without a mediator, thus falling into either atheism or deism, two things almost equally abhorrent to Christianity."

The same point is made by the contemporary Jewish philosopher of religion Julius Guttman, writing of Israel's idea of God as "not the fruit of philosophic speculation but the product of the immediacy of the religious consciousness". The decisive feature of monotheism, he writes, "is that it is not grounded in an abstract idea of God, but in an intensely powerful divine will which rules history. This implies a thoroughly personalistic conception of God ... between two moral personalities, between an 'I' and a 'Thou'."

This does not mean, of course, that philosophy has no role within religion. It means that philosophy can never be a substitute nor a complete justification for religion. It means that religion does not stand or fall by external information or external inferences, including science, any more than a love relationship is validated by factors outside a relationship and the experience of the two persons involved. A religious apprehension of God is founded on a personal relationship.

If I now single out Christianity to expand, and end, this theme, it is not to promote the claims of Christianity above other religions (angels profess no single religious confession), but because you yourself have focused your attacks principally on the Christian faith. For Christians, God does not have a more fundamental witness than Jesus Christ. What and who God is, even the fact of God's existence, is founded for Christians on the person and history of Jesus. The spiritual and ethical riches of the Christian religion, its potential for human flourishing down the ages, are not based on the boss-man God of your caricatures, but on the Christ who excoriated hypocrites and a finger-wagging priesthood; who taught care of the poor, non-reliance on possessions, and identity with the frail of the world. His triumph was not the inheritance of an earthly kingdom won and secured by military power, but his death on the cross.

Above all he preached a new notion of love, known to his followers as *agape*: a special love that is different from romantic, erotic, and familial love, in that it is entirely non-judgmental, and selfless, and graces the loved one rather than the lover. It is difficult to get through the course of a human life without making judgments on partners, spouses, children, colleagues, parents: and, in any case, such judgments are often necessary. But the virtually impossible imperative of *agape* is based on the Christian belief that all without exception have a destiny towards God irrespective of the differences between individual human beings. This means that all human beings are exalted: and the very fact of this potential to engage in the love of *agape*, non-judgmental love, increases that exaltation. It is because of the exaltation of every individual without exception that Christianity teaches respect (not merely toleration) for others, despite differences. The love of *agape* insists on engaging difference with patience, respect, and gentleness. This does not mean that a Christian should compromise on profound matters of principle; above all, it does not imply compromise on the principle of respect based on *agape* itself. But there is a deep paradox involved. For while all are deemed to be exalted, Christians accept that all are equally fallen; original sin, a term you so despise, is not a notion that people are happy with today. But one way of viewing that fallenness, that stain in human nature, is to regard it as the context in which human beings struggle to perform the difficult task of achieving non-judgmental love. It is this acknowledgment of fallenness that enables Christians to pick themselves up and to start again when they fail. This applies not just to everyday individual circumstances, but to periods of history and entire peoples. How else do Christians explain the crimes of the Crusades, the Inquisition, the wars of religion? And it is precisely the exalted yet fallen, God-centred basis of such a creed that distinguishes it from those ideologies in the modern period that are purely man-centred: Marx, Nietzsche, Freud. When man-centred philosophies fail they are thrown into the dustbin of history. Christians pick themselves up and start again.

Christians are not sustained in their God-centred humanity by ideas or sets of beliefs, any more than are Jews, Muslims, Hindus, and other religionists, who at different levels have their own notions of love of neighbour. Being religious, constantly renewing and rediscovering a personal relationship with God, involves religious practice. At the centre of all the great world religions is the practice of prayer, which has, like poetry and music, myriad varieties. You have some fun with prayer in a section you entitle "The Great Prayer Experiment", where you rightly expose empirical experiments claiming the efficacy of intercession — a sad example of how religious practice denigrates itself by seeking vindication through science.

George Herbert, the religious poet of the early seventeenth century, wrote a fine poem entitled "Prayer" that gives a rather different, expansive sense of the Christian scope and power of prayer, and thereby what it means to be religious:

> *Prayer, the Church's banquet, Angels' age,*
> *God's breath in man returning to his birth,*
> *The soul in paraphrase, heart in pilgrimage,*

The Christian plummet sounding heav'en and earth;

Engine against th' Almighty, sinner's tower,
Reversed thunder, Christ-side-piercing spear,
The six-days'-world transposing in an hour,
A kind of tune, which all things hear and fear;

Softness, and peace, and joy, and love, and bliss,
Exalted manna, gladness of the best,
Heaven in ordinary, man well dressed,
The milky way, the bird of Paradise,

Church bells beyond the stars heard, the soul's blood,
The land of spices, something understood.

A final word on the uses of imagination as a solution to the apparent antagonism between science and religion. I was impressed by your favourable citation of the theoretical physicist Lee Smolin. Smolin is obviously a thinker very close to your heart on specific issues in cosmology and biology. And now he has delivered himself, too, on the wider questions of science and philosophy. In the opening paragraph of his book *The Trouble with Physics* he encapsulates, hopefully and most generously, the multi-dimensional task of human enquiry after truth. An angel could not have put it better:

There may or may not be a God. Or gods. Yet there is something ennobling about our search for the divine. And also something humanizing, which is reflected in each of the paths people have discovered to take us to deeper levels of truth. Some seek transcendence in meditation or prayer; others seek it in service to their fellow human beings; still others, the ones lucky enough to have the talent, seek transcendence in the practice of any art. Another way of engaging life's deepest questions is science.

With affection, from Darwin's Angel, and Yours

Acknowledgments

I am greatly indebted to Nicholas Lash for encouragement, theological guidance, and suggestions throughout the text. I also have to thank John Wilkins, Tim Jenkins, Ruth Padel, Randal Keynes, Tim Lewens, Michael Burleigh, and Michael McGhee for useful comments and quotations. I am indebted to Michael Buckley SJ for ideas and quotations in the section "Being Religious". I am particularly grateful to Marilyn Robinson for highlighting the influence of John Hartung in her *Harper's Magazine* review of *The God Delusion* (November 2006) and to Ralph C. Wood for insights into Dostoyevsky on atheism in his article "Ivan Karamazov's Mistake" in *First Things*,

December 2002. For further reading I would recommend *Three Ways of Believing in God* by Nicholas Lash, *God Matters* by Herbert McCabe, *Real Presences* by George Steiner, and *At the Origins of Modern Atheism* by Michael Buckley. Finally, I wish to thank Clare Alexander, as ever, and Peter Carson.